Essential Management Models

Essential Management Models is a compilation of business tools that actually work. It's a guide to the very best in practical management thinking. No reinventing the wheel, no management fads and no corporate word-bingo.

Essential Management Models demystifies strategy tools and does so with attitude: the view that any decision is better than no decision. The book encourages you to "go on…decide" and provides you with reference on how to do so.

Rather than a series of independent summaries, the book makes connections between frameworks to expose the overlaps and relationships between them. This is the key to what makes the exercise worthwhile, the tools useful and the book unique.

Using diagrams extensively to explain key concepts, but without ever "dumbing down", the book is written for managers who get things done – or students who want to.

If you've ever studied management or strategy before, *Essential Management Models* will enable you to go back to the models and use them to do a better job, or think more clearly. It will remind you of the interlinkages between the frameworks to really make them work as a coherent whole. If you've forgotten them, it will give you confidence to use them. If you've written them off as mere theory, we urge you to think again.

Grant S. Foster ran his market strategy consulting business Ellis Foster McVeigh from 2009 to 2019. A highly sought-after educator in Melbourne, Sydney and Hong Kong, Grant had held adjunct lecturer posts with Macquarie Graduate School of Management, the Graduate School of Business at the University of Sydney, Mt Eliza Business School (now Melbourne Business School) and the Australian Graduate School of Management. Grant was a member of the Australian Institute of Company Directors and also a director of crisis support charity Lifeline Australia (mental health/suicide prevention). Prior to his consulting career, Grant was GM of Marketing and Sales for business telco Commander Australia. He had an MBA from Bond University. Grant passed away in 2019.

Chris J. Grannell has held several roles in strategy, innovation, product development and related areas. He is Chief Product Officer for education marketplace Adventus.io. He also advises several early-stage businesses and has held senior positions at Carsales.com and Solvup.com/TIC Group after working with Grant as marketing and strategy business consultant. He has an MBA from Melbourne Business School. Chris has written for the *Financial Times*, *WARC/Market Leader*, *Nine/Fairfax* and others.

"Connecting the dots between the best management theories of the past 50 years, *Essential Management Models* calls on us to 'go on… decide' and reminds us where innovation fits within the broader business context".
Tony Ulwick, Founder and CEO of Strategyn

Essential Management Models

Tried and Tested Business Frameworks for Strategy, Customers and Growth

**Grant S. Foster and
Chris J. Grannell**

"Hope is not a strategy. What's yours?"

Routledge
Taylor & Francis Group

LONDON AND NEW YORK

Cover design: David Fox

First published 2023
by Routledge
4 Park Square, Milton Park, Abingdon, Oxon OX14 4RN

and by Routledge
605 Third Avenue, New York, NY 10158

Routledge is an imprint of the Taylor & Francis Group, an informa business

British Library Cataloguing-in-Publication Data
A catalogue record for this book is available from the British Library

Library of Congress Cataloging-in-Publication Data
Names: Foster, Grant S., author. | Grannell, Chris J., author.
Title: Essential management models: tried and tested business frameworks for strategy, customers and growth / Grant S. Foster and Chris J. Grannell.
Description: Abingdon, Oxon; New York, NY : Routledge, 2022. | Includes bibliographical references and index.
Identifiers: LCCN 2021060866 (print) | LCCN 2021060867 (ebook) | ISBN 9780367481575 (hardback) | ISBN 9780367521875 (paperback) | ISBN 9781003038276 (ebook)
Subjects: LCSH: Strategic planning. | Management.
Classification: LCC HD30.28.F685 2022 (print) | LCC HD30.28 (ebook) | DDC 658.4/012—dc23/20220105
LC record available at https://lccn.loc.gov/2021060866
LC ebook record available at https://lccn.loc.gov/2021060867

ISBN: 9780367481575 (hbk)
ISBN: 9780367521875 (pbk)
ISBN: 9781003038276 (ebk)

DOI: 10.4324/9781003038276

Typeset in Univers
by codeMantra

Access the Support Material: www.routledge.com/9780367521875

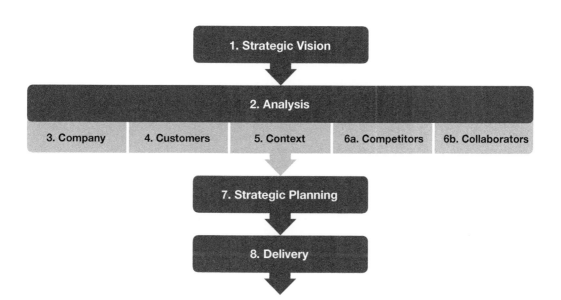

In memory of Grant

Contents

Models Featured

Foreword

What the business world needs least – another book on strategy. Remember Ansoff's Matrix? Porter's Five Forces? Do you really know what Christensen's Disruptive Innovation was about or Moore's Adoption Chasm?

If you went to business school anytime in the past 20 years or so you will recall at least a couple of these models or frameworks, and there are dozens more, but how often have you seen them since?

Specifically, how many business strategy documents have you read that use these essential tools of strategy? We've noticed in our consulting business how the word "strategy" is everywhere, but how rarely do we find any evidence of the use of the strategic tools and frameworks we learned and still teach in universities and business schools.

Management models aren't predictions; they aren't exact analogues of "real life"; and they never claimed to be accurate 100% of the time. But these frameworks were developed to help analyse competitive circumstances and alternatives in a structured way so that strategic decisions can be better informed and more effective.

This book is a practical guide. It will enable you to go back to the models and use them to do a better job, or think more clearly. It will show you the interlinkages to really make them work as a coherent whole. If you've forgotten them, it will give you confidence to use them. If you've written them off as mere theory, we urge you to think again. Used well, they will elevate business decision making from personal opinion to robust strategic plans and could change the way you do business.

This is not another book on strategy; it is a compendium of what we believe to be the best models from the best books and papers. And by "best", we mean most useful and most relevant to business today.

Each of the models and frameworks was originated and tested by leading International strategic thinkers and practitioners. We have provided a brief summary of each tool, but more importantly have included links and references to the original texts, and the website essentialmanagementmodels.com provides shortcuts to relevant sources.

■ **Foreword**

This book is designed to dip in and out of. It's a launchpad for exploring the texts further and it shows how different models connect to one another. Key concepts and cross-references are shown in **bold**. Quotations and diagrams remain the property of their respective owners and references to original sources are provided within each section.

1 Strategic Vision

What We Want to Be and Why

The Cheshire Cat told Alice if you don't know where you're going, then any road will take you there, but his advice should be noted by businesses as a reminder of where each strategic planning process should begin. If you're starting in the middle of the Australian outback, you'll need plenty of fuel, water, a map and a satnav. If your journey begins in New York, you'll need your wits about you to flag down a taxi; and in London, you'll need a Tube map.

With a core purpose clearly defined, strategy becomes about knowing where you are going (vision) and choosing which roads (strategic choices) will get you there. Without a strategic destination or ambition for the organisation, every possible choice and decision is equally valid but progress is difficult, if not impossible.

Whilst an understanding of where you *are* is essential before fleshing out a strategy (more on this in a moment), it is not unusual – *in fact some would say, essential* – to have an idea about where you want to go before you begin. We recommend using some of the tools in this section to start articulating what you want to be, as long as you come back to the vision later and update in the light of the detailed analysis that you'll undertake next.

Above all else, strategy is about making decisions. It is as much about what you decide not to do as it is about planned action. This section contains some of the best tools to help businesses make those key choices.

WHAT TO LOOK OUT FOR

Vision done badly is a waste of time. When treated as a cosmetic or superficial exercise, that's all you will get from it.

A vision is not just a luxury for "big corporates". In very small businesses, the vision resides in the head of the founder. But as soon as you have a few members of the team, it needs to be shared. It should help the organisation make decisions. It should move you forward, not simply be a reassertion of what is already obvious. Enshrined in the vision is some decision – the organisation is taking a position on how and why it will operate.

DOI: 10.4324/9781003038276-1

If your colleagues insist on using a framework that doesn't really tell you anything new, you should feel justified in pushing back. Similarly, just agreeing to *do a good job* – like *making a lot of money* or *helping people* – is neither a vision nor a strategy.

1.1 COLLINS' AND PORRAS' VISION FRAMEWORK

Many executives have been involved in fruitless discussions about "vision" and "mission" that achieve little beyond motherhood statements. This has given both a bad name.

This is a tragedy.

We find that done correctly, getting clarification on vision and direction can be one of the most valuable things that you do. NASA's 1960s vision of "putting a man on the moon by the end of the decade" is still famous for good reason. Tesla talks about "accelerating the advent of sustainable transport" and they mean it, as evidenced by making many of their patents available on an open-source basis. Australian luggage manufacturer Crumpler states it makes bags "built for purpose and made to last", and demonstrates this by designing for specific uses and users (photographers, couriers, consultants) and offering free lifetime repairs.

For successful organisations, vision is tangible. It provides measurable direction for the business and motivation and inspiration to employees, partners and team members. It's also easily understood.

If you're looking for a way to make sense of this, you could do worse than turn to the Vision Framework of Jerry Porras and Jim Collins. It features at the heart of their seminal book *Built to Last*,[1] and in contrast to much of common practice, the clarity of this approach to company vision is like a breath of fresh air.

Their vision comprises two parts – the *Core Ideology* and the *Envisioned Future*. Sounds a little esoteric? It's actually very straightforward.

- Core Ideology is the organisation's purpose and its values. In other words, the *why* and the *how*.
- Envisioned Future is about inspiring customers, partners and team members with specific goals. This is the *What*. In subsequent writings, Collins got stuck into this part of the vision with gusto, introducing the world to BHAGs (*Big Hairy Audacious Goals*).

That's it. Once the component parts have been agreed, there is simply no need to set about composing a wordy "vision statement". As Collins and Porras say, "it is about picking a goal that will stimulate change and progress, and making

---

1 Porras, J., & Collins, J., 1994, *Built to Last*, Harper Collins. Also featured in Porras, J. & Collins, J., 1996, 'Building Your Company's Vision', *Harvard Business Review*.

a resolute commitment to it. This is not about writing a mission statement. This is about going on a mission!"

Our view on the mission; use the word if it helps, but don't create another tier of complexity just for the sake of it.

Whilst so much strategy work focuses on what should be done and how, Collins adds the critical dimension of *why* we might do it in the first place. Collins and Porras' concepts "personalise" strategy for organisations and employees. Used well and communicated broadly, they can motivate, inspire and unify individuals into winning organisations.

Anyone who has seen anything by Simon Sinek (and let's face it, he's almost impossible to get away from these days) may be reminded of Sinek's dictum *Why, How, What* featured in his book *Start with Why*. Although we prefer Collins' more in-depth approach, it boils down to the same principle: start with a purpose or overarching objective and use that to create direction and discipline.

We like Collins and Porras' Vision Framework because of the balance that it brings: hard and soft, qualitative and quantitative – head and heart, so to speak. The Ying Yang symbol which they co-opt (shown in **Figure 1.1**) is very apt. Not only are the two parts complementary but there is an inherent tension between them – to set a direction, an organisation needs both a broad set of principles and a specific set of goals. Another inherent tension in their model is between continuity (values) and change (goals need to be updated). Collins and Porras

Core Ideology+ Goals = Vision

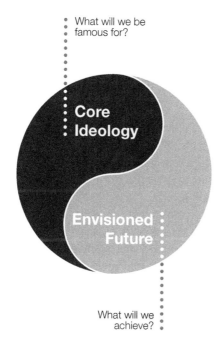

Figure 1.1
Core Ideology +
Envisioned Future
= Vision, from Built
to Last Copyright
© 1994 by Jim
Collins and Jerry
Porras Reprinted by
permission of Curtis
Brown, Ltd. All
rights reserved.

suggest that managers should adopt the mantra of "preserve the core and stimulate progress".

We also like the Core Ideology part because it additionally brings together two ideas: purpose and values. How does this fit with the other models in this book?

Well, you can't have a meaningful Purpose if you don't know what customers want – see **Model 4.5 The Job-to-be-Done and Outcome-Driven Innovation**. At a stretch, a good Purpose could be thought of as a set of jobs customers need to get done. And it closely connects to a brand essence. Collins intends Values as organisational values – behaviours to which the business ascribes. As you will see, we think these can be the same as Brand Values, see **Model 1.6 Brand Charter and Desired Reputation**.

1.2 KERNEL OF STRATEGY – RUMELT

Rumelt likes to stir the pot. His 2017 *Good Strategy/Bad Strategy*[2] broke new ground in savaging management mumbo-jumbo, and for this reason alone, it is worthy of being at the top of your reading list.

As well as roundly dismissing corporate feelgood, Rumelt also provides some of the sharpest clarity on the heart of what is, and is not, strategy. For the uninitiated, anything that looks like a wellness seminar for your organisation is *bad strategy. Good strategy*, on the other hand, is summed up by Rumelt in his *Kernel of Strategy* which has three parts:

1. Diagnosis – figuring out "what's going on here?", which includes understanding of obstacles, opportunities and competitor activity
2. Guiding Policy – an optimal approach based on the best understanding of the diagnosis
3. Set of Coherent Actions – set out in enough detail to provide direction and focus; plus ensure alignment across coordinated activities that the organisation is going to pursue

We can't do justice to the depth with which Rumelt addresses these concepts here, but the self-evident nature of the logic in this approach speaks for itself. In fact, you'll see elements of this approach reflected in the following sections: Analysis (Diagnosis) and Coherent Actions (Delivery). But these ideas aren't unique to Professor Rumelt either, as we'll see.

Rumelt isn't the only thinker to put his own spin on the loose body of strategy theories. Parallels with Collins are not hard to spot, especially in "guiding policy" which also echoes Michael Porter's seminal *What Is Strategy?*[3] in which he proposed the now-familiar dictum that strategy is as much about what you

---

2 Rumelt, R., 2017, *Good Strategy/Bad Strategy*, Profile Books.
3 Porter, M. E., 1996, 'What Is Strategy?', *Harvard Business Review*, Vol. 74, pp. 61–78.

won't do as it is about what you will. Similarities with Sinek are obvious, but Rumelt's "diagnosis" has a much more rigorous air. In a similar vein, you will find Rumelt introducing a "chain link strategy" within the Coherent Actions. This concept parallels "activity systems", see **Model 3.4 Sources of Competitive Advantage**.

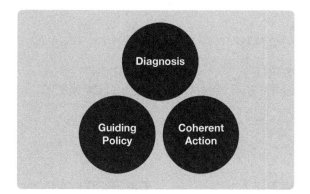

Figure 1.2
The Kernel of Strategy, Based on the Concepts Outlined in Rumelt, *Good Strategy/Bad Strategy*.

1.3 ANSOFF'S GROWTH MATRIX

Any business with shareholders needs to grow, otherwise it will die. Why? Because if it doesn't grow, then investors face the ignominy of knowing that they could have done better by putting their money in the bank instead.

That's not all. Growth is generally considered a laudable objective in all kinds of organisations – from profit-motivated corporations to strictly not-for-profit community groups. What caregiving organisation wouldn't want to provide *more* help or help *more* people in future? What government body wouldn't want to roll out its services to *more* citizens?

In short, most companies want to grow. In fact, when we interview CEOs and executives, they frequently cite growth as a core strategy for their organisation, but *growth is not a strategy*. And those who claim otherwise are seriously mistaken. Growth may be an objective. It is a possible outcome, but it is not a strategy until we answer the critical question... *how?*

Revenue growth can come by increasing prices (more on this in **Model 4.12 The Pocket Pricing Model** and **Model 4.19 Supply and Demand**), but also by selling more, servicing more – or securing more customers. And as any management group contemplates a vision for an organisation, it needs to have a handle on where it thinks growth should come from.

H. Igor Ansoff was a mathematician and an engineer, yet his Growth Matrix,[4] first published in Harvard Business Review in 1957, remains till date, in our minds, one of the most useful strategic planning tools.

---

4 Ansoff, H., September–October 1957, 'Strategies for Diversification', *Harvard Business Review*.

Ansoff tells us there are only four ways to grow.

Too simple, surely? Well no, just insightful, and if you think of a fifth we'd like to hear from you.

There are, of course, different ways to execute the Ansoff options – organically, via spin-offs, mergers and acquisitions (M&A), new distribution and channel partnerships – but always only four core strategies.

Figure 1.3
Ansoff's Matrix.

EXISTING PRODUCTS/SERVICES   NEW PRODUCTS/SERVICES

EXISTING MARKETS

MARKET PENETRATION
- New users
- New usage
- More usage

PRODUCT DEVELOPMENT
- New product development
- Product or range extensions
- Complementary offers

NEW MARKETS

MARKET DEVELOPMENT
- New geographic markets
- New market segments

DIVERSIFICATION
- Related or unrelated

FOUR WAYS TO GROW THE BUSINESS

A few points to consider:

- A viable growth strategy may feature activity in more than one quadrant, but beware of the plan that features a smorgasbord of options in all four.
- Many businesses and individuals find the idea of new products, new markets or diversification much more appealing than the hard grind of market penetration.
- Has the business done all it can to optimise its returns in current products and markets? Is it possible that a renewed focus and investment on Market Penetration would yield the best returns and lowest risk?
- Is the current market growing or has it reached its peak? Can it support the future growth ambitions of the business? Is it time to think beyond "business as usual" and explore new opportunities?
- Do existing customer relationships and business competencies present an opportunity to offer new products or services more effectively than those currently available?
- Is the business capable of spreading its skills, attention and resources beyond its existing activities?

1.4 THE GROWTH-SHARE MATRIX

Also known as the BCG Matrix in honour of the Boston Consulting Group where it originated, this framework[5] combines market share with market growth to provide direction for strategic investment in business units (or products or brands) that are likely to have a competitive advantage.

The Growth-Share Matrix is frequently used with **Model 1.3 Ansoff's Matrix** to explore how a firm can maintain growth or sow the seeds of the next phase of growth in the face of flagging or maturing products.

The "cash flow" arrow in our diagram indicates that funds generated by the cash cow should be invested into the "question mark" with the intention of turning it into a "star". If this feels a little simplistic, that's because it is.

The model makes assumptions that are far from universally applicable. It also ignores relevant issues other than the two represented, which means it is a useful *starting point* for discussion but should not be followed blindly.

Here are a few points to ponder:

- The BCG Matrix is a snapshot of past performance that ignores trends. Is the market share of the *Star* trending up or down? Is the *Question Mark* any more or less questionable than it was six months ago? Is the *Cash Cow* market stable or disappearing?
- Strategy is about making decisions for the future so that the direction of each business unit concerning the four quadrants is critical.
- The Matrix assumes that market dominance is a competitive and commercial advantage.
- Sometimes being small and nimble is a competitive advantage (see **Model 3.4 Sources of Competitive Advantage**).
- It assumes that business units operate relatively independently – perhaps the *Dog* is needed to support other activities?
- It assumes that the firm can correctly diagnose when a question mark has turned irrevocably into a Dog. Billions of dollars are wasted each year funding projects which are doomed to failure. Conversely, products can be killed early by being starved of investment.

1.5 MCKINSEY'S ATTRACTIVENESS-STRENGTHS MATRIX

The Attractiveness-Strengths Matrix[6] was McKinsey & Co.'s embellishment on the BCG Matrix. It gives us an alternative means of considering strategic opportunities. It combines attractiveness with corporate strengths instead of the axes of growth and market share.

---

5 Henderson, B., January 1970, *The Product Portfolio*, The Boston Consulting Group, Boston.
6 Various, *McKinsey & Company*, 1970s onwards.

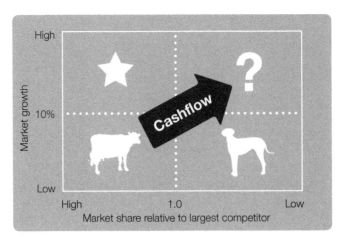

Figure 1.4
BCG Matrix.

The way to use the tool is largely self-evident – as a guide only. As before, the only risk is in taking the tool too seriously. Like the BCG Matrix before, it can be helpful in shaping and presenting our thinking as we build business strategies. But tools like these must not be relied upon to make the strategic decision on your behalf – that is the job of the strategist. Be careful! Measures on dimensions are not objective – they rely heavily on opinion and can be influenced by the bias of the user.

The market attractiveness relates to the environment. It helps to remember that when an overall market is growing, everyone in the market can grow without needing to take a share from each other, making the market particularly attractive.

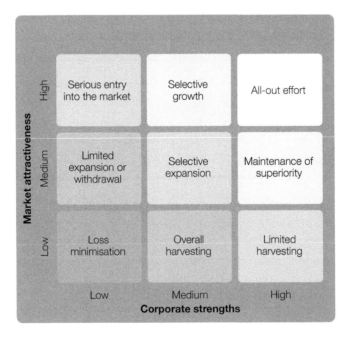

Figure 1.5
McKinsey Matrix.

Loss minimisation often takes the form of divestment. Overall harvesting suggests that only "just enough" will be spent on the business and its revenue subject to a "harvesting" (rather than investment) approach. It would be treated as a kind of cash cow.

Selective treatment is spent on the diagonal (serious entry, selective expansion and limited harvesting.

1.6 BRAND CHARTER AND DESIRED REPUTATION

We're not too sure when the term Brand Charter began, but it's a good name for a concept that seems to have emerged in Australia during the 1990s and no one claims to have a monopoly on its use.

Brand Pyramids, Brand Onions, Brand Butterflies – every book, every paper, every branding agency has seen the need to build its own model. This is a large part of the problem with branding in business today – the lack of a common language – which as a consequence has led to the status and role of brand in corporate strategy being diminished.

The Brand Charter model that we use draws on the work of many academics and practitioners. It's the model that Grant taught in MBA programmes in Australia and Hong Kong, and we've used it in our consulting business. Today it's widely used by leading organisations in Australia and overseas.

In theory, it's pretty simple. Identify the *essence of the brand* – when everything else is stripped away, this must answer the question – "what does this brand stand for?". Then define the three or four behaviours that will collectively deliver the Brand Essence, and in doing so, define and differentiate the business. You can think of it this way: "The brand values clarify and substantiate the essence".

Sometimes when a business contemplates a new venture, division or line, it finds that this doesn't fit with the associations of the brand. When a brand won't "stretch", it may be a clue that you shouldn't be doing it; or it may be a cue to use a different brand for this part of the organisation. More on this in **Model 7.4 Brand Architecture**.

Brand essence and values are expected to be a little aspirational (they are supposed to inspire after all), but they also need more than a grain of truth. We sometimes say that the Brand Charter is the Desired Reputation of the organisation.

A little experiment you can run with your colleagues – whether from your local sports club, charitable foundation or major corporation – is to pick a couple of competitors and attempt to write out *their* Brand Charter. Then show it to colleagues. Can they recognise the company from the words alone? The exercise demonstrates that brands are about *reputation*, but it also highlights whether organisations are clones of each other and whether they are clear about what they want to stand for.

Does Brand Charter fit within the Vision of the organisation? We're pleased you asked – *yes*. Brand Essence and Values absolutely can be part of the company vision. As Collins and Porras' Vision Framework reminds us (see **Model 1.1**), a vision comprises both the *what* and the *why*, and the Brand Charter is a perfect articulation of the latter.

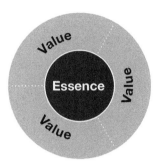

Figure 1.6
Brand Charter:
Essence and
Values.

Many organisations have focused on creating a consistent brand image. Whether or not these brands appeal to us as individuals, we can see that they stand for something. Think of Virgin (irreverent people's champion), BMW (the joy of the ultimate driving machine), New Zealand (100% pure), Body Shop (inner beauty and wellbeing that doesn't cost the Earth), Trumpism (sticking it up to the established way of doing things), Mini (cheeky and fun to drive), The British Royal Family….?

And finally, a word or two of warning. When you think of brand as *desired reputation*, we will clearly have a problem if it only has a life within the marketing department. By analogy, profitability isn't just an exercise for the finance department, just as strategy isn't just the responsibility of the strategy team. A brand strategy should *inform and sit above* communications or messages, which are tactics or tools to deliver the desired result.

2   Analysis

We start our journey here.

There is an old Irish joke about the man who asks for directions to Dublin and is told "if I was going to Dublin, I wouldn't be starting from here". The strategic planning process encourages all kinds of grand visions and ambitious plans, but there is one constant – we have little choice about where we start.

Whether a global corporation or an embryonic start-up, we begin here, where we are, with what we have. Nothing more – nothing less. The question for every business at this point is "*What does 'here' look like?*"

So how might we answer that seemingly simple question?

We suggest a mix of internal and external analysis. We've included some frameworks that should help you work out where to focus effort and attention in order to gain a comprehensive understanding of the context in which the strategic vision will be pursued.

In this book, we have presented Vision before Analysis. This is deliberate because it reflects how most organisations or products are conceived. Of course, the founders of a company or those commissioning the project reckon they have some idea about the market before they start – and the tools in the previous section should help you structure your ideas. But once your analysis is done – once you've learnt more about what 'here' looks like – it's essential that vision is updated to suit. In John Maynard Keynes' immortal line, "When the facts change, I change my mind – what do you do, sir?"

When we teach this in MBA programmes we refer to the 5 C's. After presenting a few overarching analysis frameworks we'll address each in turn:

- Company
- Customers
- Context
- Competitors
- Collaborators

DOI: 10.4324/9781003038276-2   **11** □

WHAT TO LOOK OUT FOR

During any type of analysis, stay alert for opinion masquerading as fact. Effective strategy demands facts – sometimes brutal, but always robust and able to be substantiated.

If a big issue is identified and whiteboarded, don't ignore it! Keep it with you, like a nagging voice on your shoulder, as you proceed to build up your strategy.

The importance of hunting down facts doesn't mean you should keep looking for them if they don't exist yet. This can lead to analysis paralysis. Sometimes you don't know for certain – and can't. In this situation, we urge you to *do something*. In cases like these, you can usually process slowly, generate facts as you do so, and change direction or evolve as the results come in. Companies that cultivate an ability to move *when they know enough* can turn this into a source of advantage.

2.1 SWOT

We couldn't write about analysis without including the SWOT tool, but we thought about it.

SWOT is an acronym for Strengths, Weaknesses (internal issues over which you have direct control), Opportunities and Threats (external issues that impact your business).

SWOT is ubiquitous – the one tool that's almost always present in a business plan and the most commonly used one when the CEO pulls the team into an executive retreat. Unfortunately, it is almost always misused to the point we issue this warning: **beware of SWOT**. This is not just our opinion. There was a study in 1999 which showed that companies that used SWOT as their primary planning tool revealed a negative relationship with performance.[1]

Now before you go burning your existing strategic plan, let us explain how it is misused, and more importantly, how it can be used to good effect.

Two major factors contribute to its misuse. The first is the tendency for it to become a list of unsubstantiated opinions, rather than facts supported by evidence and data. It is alarming how "Great People", "Strong Relationships", "Best Products" and "Powerful Brand" become enshrined as strengths of a business, just because it seemed like the right thing to say and they were categorised as such in a SWOT workshop exercise. We'll return to the idea of fake strengths in **Model 3.1 Capabilities and Core Competences**. Strategy cannot be based on

---

1 Menon, A., Bharadwaj, S. G., Adidam, P. T., & Edison, S. W., 1999, 'Antecedents and Consequences of Marketing Strategy Making', *Journal of Marketing*, Vol. 63, No. 2, pp. 18–40.

opinion, on what people want to hear, or worse still, on wishes and hope. SWOT reviews are no exception.

The second and in our minds more significant concern with the use of SWOT is that it tends to be used as a general overview and assessment of a business, rather than as an aid to considering a specific strategic objective.

A generic SWOT review of say, Tesco, would read very differently if the strategy under consideration was to launch into India. A SWOT of Manchester United would be very different if its strategy involved the creation of an NBL side versus an expansion of the soccer franchise into China. The issues SWOT must address are the Strengths, Weaknesses, Opportunities and Threats that exist for a specific organisation as it contemplates a specific course of action.

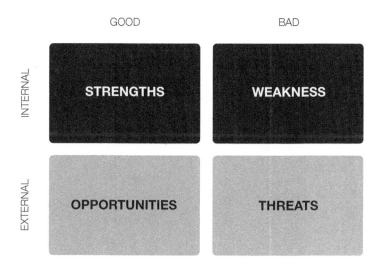

Figure 2.1
SWOT Analysis.

Be suspicious of the SWOT review (it's not an analysis when it has no context) that sits at the beginning of the business plan and is unrelated to specific strategy goals and objectives. It is at best useless and may be unhelpfully misleading.

On the other hand, if it is based on facts, rather than opinion and refers directly to the internal and external factors related to a specific strategy proposal – the Diagnosis in Rumelt's model – it might just be worth doing.

2.2 COLLINS' HEDGEHOG CONCEPT

If we are sounding like Jim Collins fans, we are. The Hedgehog concept is another tool for framing your thinking.

The Hedgehog Concept is not about setting a goal to be the best – it is about understanding and single-mindedly pursuing that which a business can be best at.

In *Good to Great*,[2] Collins identified the common capacity of great companies to have a deep understanding of three things:

- An understanding that nothing great can be accomplished without passion, so they limit their primary arenas of activity to those for which they have great passion.
- They know what they can be the best in the world at. Whilst "best in the world" might be local or highly focused, for example, "best in the world at providing home care for the people of Adelaide, South Australia", it nonetheless captures what they can do better than any other institution on the planet.
- An understanding of what best drives their economic or resource engine. A for-profit business might identify one economic denominator – profit per X – that has the most significant impact on its economics. A social sector organisation could determine how best to improve its total resource engine (volunteers, government support) so that it spends less time worrying about money and more time fulfilling its core purpose.

As Collins writes "It takes discipline to say 'no, thank you' to big opportunities. The fact that something is a 'once-in-a-lifetime opportunity' is irrelevant if it doesn't fit within the three circles".[3]

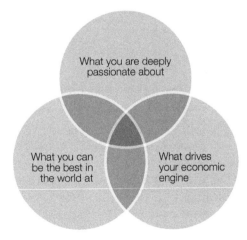

Figure 2.2
Collins' Hedgehog Concept from Good to Great Copyright © 2001 by Jim Collins Reprinted by permission of Curtis Brown, Ltd. All rights reserved.

2.3 THE VALUE CHAIN

The value chain is a very simple concept.

Any finished product or service is the end result of several stages of processing, manufacturing or enhancement. In our visualisation in **Figure 2.3**, products flow from left to right. (Money flows in the opposite direction from right to left.)

---

2 Collins, J., 2006, *Good to Great*, Random House, London.
3 Collins, J., 2001, *Good to Great*, p. 136.

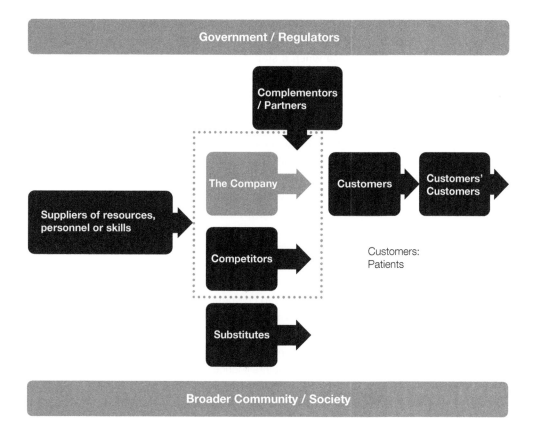

Figure 2.3
The Value Chain.
This Diagram
Builds Upon the
Ideas Expressed by
Various Authors.

A customer is defined as a party that pays money for something and a supplier is defined as a party that receives money in exchange for goods or services.

At any stage in the value chain, the difference between the cost of the inputs and the price of the outputs is the gross profit margin: namely, revenue minus cost of goods sold.

Value chain analysis starts by identifying what the stages for a particular industry are and then seeks to place the appropriate organisations in the relevant boxes. A more comprehensive examination may determine the margin for each stage in the chain.

Things to look out for:

- In mature markets, a single company will often pop up at multiple points in the value chain. In other words, a particular firm may be both a supplier and a substitute at the same time.
- Integration (also known as "vertical integration") occurs when neighbouring steps in the chain are merged, as when a retailer buys a manufacturer or vice versa. Many e-commerce giants have deployed integration strategies – such as when Amazon created products for sale on its own platform (Amazon makes goods for sale, so does Facebook). Companies pursuing

this approach need to be careful around the thorny issue of self-preferencing in order to stay on the right side of competition regulations.

- Disintermediation takes place when a step in the value chain is cut out. Most famously this occurs when a manufacturer begins to sell directly to end consumers, typically using an online store to bypass traditional channels to market. Also known as D2C or "Direct to Consumer".

- Reintermediation (like Countermediation, which we'll see next) is a relatively new phenomenon and is also largely driven by the Internet. The former refers to the creation of new intermediaries in sectors that had become predominately direct markets. This typically occurs because consumers are overwhelmed or confused by choice, which explains why they are some-times known as aggregators. Examples from the finance industry include iSelect (Australia), Money Supermarket (UK) and Coverhound (USA).

- Countermediation occurs (usually online) when an organisation operates a separate brand downstream of itself. Countermediators sometimes dis-close their parentage but can be branded separately. They typically maintain a degree of neutrality by passing clients to competitors as well as to their parents. In these cases, their role is as much about market intelligence as it is about a source of leads. Turning again to finance, the UK comparison site screentrade.com was purchased by bank Lloyds TSB in 2001 as an attempt to secure access to demand and market intelligence.

Unfortunately, the journey from left to right within a specific industry is described as a "vertical" one, but there's not much we – or anyone else – can do about it.

The Value Chain is most commonly associated with Michael Porter[4] (more on him in the next section) but has also been addressed by many other writers, particularly about the impact of the Internet.[5]

2.4 PORTER'S FIVE FORCES

Michael Porter's Five Forces model[6] was designed as an indication of the profit-ability of an industry, not (as is commonly thought) as a guide for the analysis of a specific company.

Strong forces reduce profitability. Remember that and you've got the gist of it. Porter claims that the model has been shown empirically to be a good indica-tion of long-term profitability. So, stronger bargaining power from suppliers or buyers, stronger threats of new entrants, or greater availability of substitutes means reduced profits for all in the industry.

---

4 Porter, M. E., 1985, *Competitive Advantage: Creating and Sustaining Superior Performance*, Free Press, New York and Porter, M. E., 1980, *Competitive Strategy*, Free Press, New York.

5 Chaffey, D., Ellis-Chadwick, F., Johnstone, K., & Mayer, R., 2008, *Internet Marketing: Strategy, Implementation and Practice*, 4th edn, FT Prentice Hall, London.

6 Porter, M. E., 1979, 'How Competitive Forces Shape Strategy', *Harvard Business Review*, pp. 137–145; Porter, M. E., 1980, *Competitive Strategy*, Free Press, New York, pp. 3–5; Porter, M. E., 2008, *The Five Competitive Forces That Shape Strategy*, Harvard Business.

It is perhaps surprising that industry attractiveness seems to bear little connection to the model. For example, investors continue to pour into airlines or cars whilst avoiding sectors where the Five Forces are weak such as soft drinks. As Porter himself has observed; "sexiness or hotness or coolness has nothing to do with industry profitability".

Often overlooked is the fact that the Five Forces model is designed to fit into any point along the value chain. Components and products flow from left to right, direct competitors occupy the same point in the value chain and new entrants and substitutes threaten to disrupt things from the sidelines at any moment.

The Five Forces are intended as a dynamic model, so it is important when using the tool to think not only about current performance but also in terms of the pace and direction of change. Notice how this is echoed in **Model 6.2 The Half-Truth of First Mover Advantage**.

Perhaps controversially, Porter didn't include the role of partners or Complementors in his model. In a 2008 interview on the 30th anniversary of the Five Forces,[7] he defended this move saying that "Complements are not a sixth force determining industry profitability since the presence of strong complements is not necessarily bad (or good) for industry profitability. Complements affect profitability through the way they influence the five forces".

For more on Complementors, see the **Model 6.3 Value Net**, and for more on how the web has impacted these forces, see **Model 4.15 The Long Tail**.

Figure 2.4
Porter's Five Forces, Showing Upstream, Downstream and the Current and Potential Market. Adapted with permission of Harvard Business Publishing from "How competitive forces shape strategy", *Harvard Business Review*, March–April 1979. Copyright ©1979 Harvard Business Publishing; all rights reserved.

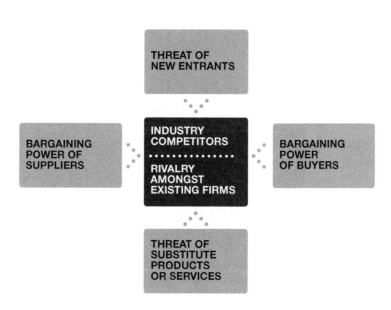

7 Porter, M.E., video interview, YouTube, 30 June 2008, viewed May 2021, http://youtube.com/watch?v=mYF2_FBCvXw

The lesson of the Five Forces echoes down the years: whilst it's easy to get distracted by the proximity of existing competitors, any strategic analysis must go broader; one pities the modern European or American car company that faces all Five Forces strongly. At the heart, there's ferocious rivalry from other vehicle brands, but over the horizon are a flurry of newcomers – both new manufacturers that look like them and companies entering from other industries. Meanwhile, alternatives to car purchase come in the form of ride-sharing, car-pooling, car-as-a-service subscriptions, and even work-from-home alternatives to the standard commute. Component manufacturers get more deeply involved in production lines and product innovation to improve their position; customers' decreasing brand loyalty means they push harder for a bargain.

2.5 MARKET FAILURE

A useful concept to bear in mind (especially for those steeped in so-called Rationalist Economics) is the idea of market failure.

When markets fail, goods aren't distributed in a way that creates the best outcome for the group. Is that open to some interpretation? Well, yes. Sometimes it is little more than a value judgement. *I don't like that outcome, so I'll call it a market failure!*

Market failure is frequently used as a political stick to beat opponents and so there is frequently disagreement about what constitutes a market failure. (Poorly paid nurses or early childcare workers are often-cited examples of economic undervaluation; many economic rationalists would disagree, pointing out that – manipulative as it sounds – people with a vocation are not likely to find substitute employment as tempting.)

Markets generally fail when

- The businesses in them are "too big to fail", and hence get propped up, when without support they would have been forced to close. Some people would say that banks being bailed out by government intervention during the Global Financial Crisis of 2007–2008 is an example of this.
- Some outputs of the organisations are not part of the market; they are external to the system of checks and balances and not factored in into financial costs. Waste – both as a by-product of production and as disposal – are examples. The growing unrepairability of consumer goods that exacerbates obsolescence is arguably a magnifying force.
- A need is so costly to fulfil, or so risky, or customers are so fragmented, that it goes unaddressed. Note how this problem can be mitigated with Internet-enabled economics as discussed in **Model 4.15 The Long Tail**.

Market failure is often used to refer to specific concepts where there are some costs or benefits that have been overlooked. Closely related are the concepts of **Externality** and the **Tragedy of the Commons**, which have been used to explain how many businesses throughout the 19th and 20th centuries were deemed "successful" while they damaged the very world that they were a part of.

3   Analysis / Company

A company or a firm is a group of people and processes working together. We tend to think of companies as if they are independent entities – *Google is good at data; SpaceX is good at rocket engineering; GE is good at solving complex everyday problems*.

It sounds obvious and perhaps it is, but knowing who you are and getting an objective view of your capabilities, isn't easy.

Tools in this section help managers think about the company itself. How does it currently operate? Where do its strengths lie? How has it been successful in the past? What sort of market opportunities is it best suited to capture?

The following sections are – in our humble opinion – the most useful tools for thinking about the Company part of your Analysis.

WHAT TO LOOK OUT FOR

Companies can succumb to their own pitches – convinced that they are better or more attractive than they actually are. Sometimes this overinflated self-importance can translate into downplaying the role of timing or accident in past success.

Push for answers to difficult questions. How do the parts of the organisation work together? In fact, do they? Does the company have a moat? (If so, does competitive advantage come from structure, capabilities or activity systems?)

Is the company prepared for multiple horizons? Or is it obsessed about a particular timeframe (either short- or long-term) at the expense of others? Do the competences that the company has allow it to jump into new markets – are they as relevant in the future as they were in the past?

Alternatively, be wary of the "fantasy scenario". If you're told that every capability is a core competence or that the company is perfectly set up to serve the market, or there are vast synergistic benefits across business units, you should feel justified to raise an eyebrow and look a little deeper.

DOI: 10.4324/9781003038276-3

3.1 CAPABILITIES AND CORE COMPETENCES

What is your organisation actually good at?

There isn't an agreed definition, but you can think of core competences as skills or proficiencies of an organisation that it does better than the competition, *and* which are difficult to replicate *and* are valuable to customers (or to the organisation itself).

To stretch a point, organisations frequently talk about *proposed* competences in which they *intend* to outperform their peers by prioritising them above other areas – to these a healthy dose of scepticism is advised.

In 1990, Hamel and Prahalad proposed that competency-based thinking be seen as a superior alternative to a business-unit view of the enterprise.[1] They suggested that core competences[2] be conceived as the "roots of a tree" from which a variety of different branches could grow.

At least that's the theory.

In practice there are a couple of problems;

- First, companies are apt to misidentify their core competences – claiming that things are "better" than they actually are, perhaps as a result of an executive defending their pitch or wishing to spotlight a pet project. As Cyne, Hall and Clifford write, "Core competence has too often become a 'feel-good' exercise that no one fails".[3]
- Second, even where competency is outstanding, results might be incorrectly attributed to it. Good outcomes might stem from something else entirely – either inside the organisation or even external to it. After a period of success, firms are most likely to attribute good results to internal (rather than external) forces, regardless of the actual cause.

It is clear that there's something in the whole idea of capabilities or competences though – it is self-evident that the skills or abilities that can give rise to one product line could be readily deployed to create another; that an organisation with strength in one area can extend into another area (indeed this is the very essence of synergy as outlined in **Model 3.6 Synergy... or Not?**.

If we define a company in terms of what it's particularly good at – rather than its business units – then it's easier to identify how we might exploit company strengths to grow in new areas. It also avoids the "bounded innovation" that tends to occur when managers work within silos.

---

1 Prahalad, C. K., & Hamel, G., 1990, 'The Core Competence of the Corporation', *Harvard Business Review*, Vol. 68, No. 3, pp. 79–91.

2 "Is it Competences" or "Competencies?" asked one of our proofreaders. It turns out that there isn't a simple answer to this question as the body of knowledge vacillates between the two. Some writers have them as synonyms; others do not.

3 Coyne, K. P., Hall, S. J. D., & Clifford, P. G., 1997, 'Is Your Core Competence a Mirage?', *McKinsey Quarterly*, Vol. 1, 40–54.

To simply say that Apple was good at creating personal computers or mobile phones would miss a significant part of what makes the organisation a force to be reckoned with. As Stalk, Evans and Shulman write,

> As a unit of analysis, new product development is too narrow. It is only part of what is necessary to satisfy a customer and, therefore, to build an organisational capability. Better to think in terms of new product realisation, a capability that includes the way a product is not only developed, but also marketed and serviced.[4]

It is perhaps ironic, given Hamel and Prahalad's desire to avoid constrained thinking, that an obsession with core competences is sometimes blamed for limiting innovation. A competence that has been relevant to a market need in the past cannot always be relied upon into the future.

The misattribution of core competences applies to competitors as much as it does to our own organisations. During consulting projects, we came across more than one organisation where the management was convinced that their rival's success was due to "a strong brand". *If only we had a single-minded brand strategy like them, we would win like them.* Occasionally, this might be true. But by overlooking competences in unsexy areas like logistics or supply chains, these managers oversimplified what was going on in their market and fundamentally missed where they would need to invest in order to compete effectively.

We'll meet the concept of a brand as an asset in **Model 4.7 Sources of Brand Equity**. A particularly insidious trap for managers is to jump from observed behaviour to the confusion that their brand is itself a core competence (or a key strength in their SWOT Analysis – **Model 2.1**). It's important to remember that consumers voting on their feet don't necessarily imply the presence of brand equity. Consumers in the mood for trial may well experiment with an unusual or novel product, even if they have little in the way of an attachment or positive opinion of it.

Even if you don't quite buy the concept of a "core" competence, the notion of a capability for an organisation can be useful. What are the skills a company needs in order to service a particular market, offer particular services or run a particular suite of products? The desired capability map can then be subject to a readiness assessment – or a gap analysis to determine where new hires, alliances or partnerships could be productive.

We will return to core competences in **Model 3.4 Sources of Competitive Advantage** where we'll see that competences are one of several ingredients that can give an organisation the edge over time.

---

4 Stalk, G., Evans, P., & Shulman, L., 1992, 'Competing on Capabilities', *Harvard Business Review*.

3.2 MCKINSEY 7-S FRAMEWORK

The McKinsey 7-S Framework is more of an aide-memoire than anything else.

It was allegedly used by new McKinsey recruits when structuring their reports on companies. The model had its first public outing in a 1980 article *Structure Is Not Organisation*[5] by Bob Waterman, Julien Phillips and Tom Peters (the latter before he acquired a "!" at the end of his name). Waterman and Peters subsequently went on to write *In Search of Excellence.*[6]

The fact that "Shared Values" appears in the centre of the diagram is no accident.

McKinsey's early managing director Marvin Bower was a keen believer in values-based management and you will see this is a trait he shares with some of our favourite management thinkers such as Collins and Aaker. Peters subsequently spoke about the "primacy" of the "Soft-Ss" (Style, Staff, Skills, Shared values) in terms of getting things done – a belief now widespread but at the time controversial.

Addressing those who may be instantly suspicious of the extreme level alliteration in the diagram, Peters attributed much of its longevity to this trick.[7] Although "corny", the seven "S"s at its heart has helped consultants, managers and CEOs remember it for 30 years.

Each "S" can be regarded as a component of the enterprise – or as a lens through which to think about the firm. The lesson here is simple – regardless of which strategic planning frameworks you use, be sure the business strategy addresses each of the Seven.

Structure, Systems, Style, Staff and Skills as tools through which a chosen strategy may be executed crop up again within **Model 3.4 Sources of Competitive Advantage**.

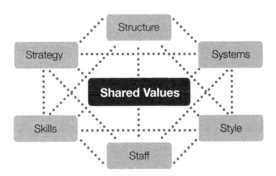

Figure 3.1
The McKinsey
Seven-S Analysis
Framework.

5 Waterman, B., Peters, T., & Phillips, J., 1980, 'Structure Is Not Organization', *Business Horizons*, Vol. 23, pp. 14–26.

6 Peters, T., & Waterman, R., 1982, *In Search of Excellence: Lessons from America's Best-run Companies*, Harper & Row, New York.

7 Peters, T., 2011, *A Brief History of the 7-S Model*, https://tompeters.com/2011/03/a-brief-history-of-s0the-7-s-mckinsey-7-s-model/.

3.3 BUSINESS STRATEGY TYPOLOGY

In their 1978 work on business typology,[8] Miles, Snow, Meyer and Coleman categorised companies by the way they respond to their markets and how they define their entrepreneurial problem or opportunity. There are four types – three of which involve coordinated, strategic choice; a fourth which is accidental and internally inconsistent.

Defenders are characterised by internal stability and are best suited to external environments that are stable too. They thrive with low variability, perhaps a single core technology or product set, where they can dominate a market or submarket (see **Model 5.4 Blank's Market Types** for more on this). Defenders "…define their entrepreneurial problem as how to seal off a portion of the total market in order to create a stable domain." They tend to focus on reliability, efficiency and market penetration, preferring to pursue business from existing or similar customers first. They are typically better marketers than the competition and offer better service though not necessarily better product quality. Their efficiency orientation means an inward focus on process, cost management and centralised control. Their approach to HR is described as "traditional" or "hierarchical".

Prospectors are internally dynamic. They are very responsive to the external environment and thrive on innovation. The typical Prospector will "… define its entrepreneurial problem as how to locate and develop product and market opportunities. The Prospector's domain is usually broad and in a continuous state of development". Prospectors are pioneers, innovators, entrepreneurs, risk-takers and opportunity seekers. They may or may not be strong in marketing or general management and are less forward integrated than a defender. They make better use of market research, testing and user feedback. Innovation may take the Prospector away from its current technical capability, and new developments tend to be market-centric rather than technology-centric. Since Prospectors are not built for routine, fixed processes, their management style tends to be less formal, favouring self-directed, internally motivated employees. In a Prospector organisation, the role of the boss is to set direction and remove impediments for employees rather than to command and control.

Analysers are a deliberate blend of Defender and Prospector, aiming to get the benefits of both with a mix of stable and dynamic approaches. They focus on a tried and trusted stable set of products, but will follow innovators. Their organisational focus tends to operate on a similar set of assumptions to that of the Prospector, but they are less willing to embrace risk. Analysers will have a degree of variety within the ranks – particularly between core business and newer product or brand extensions – but the difference is clear and the decisions

---

8 Miles, R., Snow, C., Meyer, A., & Coleman, H., 1978, 'Organizational Strategy, Structure and Process', *Academy of Management Review*, Vol. 3, No. 3, pp. 546–562.

involved are considered and deliberate. Analysers might be described as "fast followers" – they are playing catch-up to the Prospectors, but with the benefits of a large, stable base on which to draw.

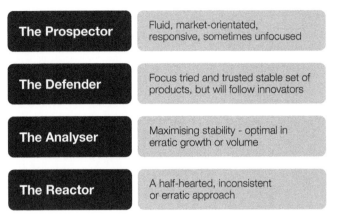

Figure 3.2
Business Strategy Typology. You Don't Want to Be a Reactor. This Figure Builds upon the Ideas Expressed in Miles et al. (1978).

Reactors are a mess. No organisation would choose to be a Reactor, which is a likely outcome of failing to move decisively. A Reactor responds poorly or chaotically to what happens in its environment. (Somewhat paradoxically given its name, the Reactor demonstrates an inability to *react* appropriately!)

Why do organisations become a Reactor? The authors cite three reasons; all of which are to do with a lack of alignment:

- Strategy is unclear or uncommunicated
- Strategy is equivocal and lacks follow-through; so, while the organisation claims it is committed to one approach, it has elements of others within its structure
- Strategy hasn't been updated in the light of changed market conditions. While individuals or teams may have begun to switch to a new operating model, the rump of the organisation is left behind and the mismatch just makes cooperation harder

Although Miles, Snow, Meyer and Coleman's taxonomy has fallen out of common use, we think it's worthy of a reboot. And it has reverberated down the generations. There are echoes of the model in the Generic Value Propositions that we meet in **Model 7.2 The Discipline of Market Leaders**, where the Prospector is reflected in the innovation of the *Product Leadership* proposition and the Defender in the low variability *Operational Excellence* proposition.

3.4 SOURCES OF COMPETITIVE ADVANTAGE

Competitive Advantage is typically about accessing lower costs (perhaps through scale, or vertical integration or tied supplies), or having different capabilities or through offering some kind of enhanced value to customers.

There are lots of organisations that have little idea of where their competitive advantage comes from – or how they might develop one in future.

Too many believe that simply doing things well will have customers queuing at their door.

The trouble is that *doing things well is not a strategy* and as competition intensifies, firms tend to learn from each other, so that "best practice" today is "common practice" tomorrow.

It's the nature of competition: Other firms will undercut, offer better services, improved products, greater convenience and generally do all they can to steal your customers. It seems they never sleep, and collectively at least – they don't.

Ideally, business strategies will identify a competitive advantage for the firm that has some degree of sustainability. While it may not last forever, true competitive advantage will give one firm an edge over the competition and the business strategy should seek to leverage and prolong that advantage. Advantages of this sort are sometimes called "moats". In a minority of cases, competitive advantage can be *formally* protected – such as with a patent – but this turns out to be rare. (Patents can be gotten around and are time-limited.) We've focused on *informal* protection – where competitive advantage is difficult to imitate or replicate for other reasons.

Moats can be created when organisations possess combinations of abilities, relationships or activities which are mutually supportive and difficult to copy; or involve trade-offs that are uncomfortable for competitors. Regarding the latter, strategists sometimes talk about decisions that have "no undo": once you're committed, you can't pull out. From the perspective of the would-be copier, choices of this sort are deeply difficult – even if you can see the logic of shutting down a particular opening to focus exclusively on another to emulate a rival, it means *giving up on something else*, and that's hard.

A key question to ask is whether these advantages are "sustainable". In truth, probably none of them are – at least not without work.

Competitive Advantage comes in broadly three forms:

1. **Structural advantages** prop up firms that dominate their markets. They include the industry "forces" analysed in Porter's Five Forces (see **Model 2.4**), but they also cover intellectual property, brands and endowments to which competitors have limited access.

   Structural advantages (also known as positional advantages) include proprietary assets, brand/reputation, tied suppliers, tied customers or anything which may alter the cost base of the company – such as scale or vertical integration (see **Model 2.3 The Value Chain**).

   Most of the points here can be considered *resource-based* – meaning that they are based on what the company does, rather than its environment. Others come in the form of endowments or government protections.

2. **Core Competences and Capabilities**

   This section is largely about management capabilities. The terms "competence" and "capability" are sometimes used interchangeably, but generally it is only the best capabilities that are regarded as competences. We met these already in **Model 3.1 Capabilities and Core Competences**.

Core competences may include innovation, marketing and relationship management, research, regulatory management and government relations, joint ventures and partnering, people and culture, systems and technology, operations, finance and investment, production and logistics.

The notion of tied customers is particularly interesting and has been responsible for the rise of more than one tech firm in recent years. In these cases, customers are rarely *actually* tied in via a contract. This type of sticky relationship is often achieved by operating as a "de facto standard". During the 1990s and early 2000s, Microsoft ran the near-ubiquitous .doc and .xls formats, and the software required to use them. In the agile project management space, Atlassian has come to dominate online kanban and scrum management with its Jira system.

3. **Activity Systems**

Closely related to core competences and capabilities are activity systems. These networks or webs of interrelated abilities, relationships or areas of focus are typically difficult for competitors to copy. Porter named them Activity Systems; Rumelt has a similar concept but refers to it as Chain-Link logic. Activities are the building blocks of systems. You can think of activities as clustering into capabilities, but in a system, they cluster in a way that is mutually reinforcing. Activities are linked potentially across the border of the organisation, reaching out to other firms, partners or communities. We've included a simplified activity system for vaccine development in **Figure 3.3**.

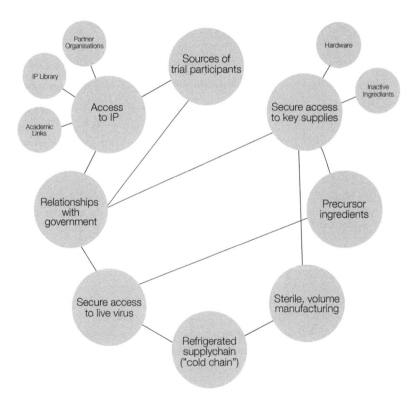

Figure 3.3 Activity System for Vaccine Development. Perhaps this Explains Why Many Covid Vaccines Were Developed by Consortia to Maximise Access to These Complementary Assets and Capabilities?

What's powerful about activity systems?

First, they appear ambiguous. It's often not quite clear from outside the organisation exactly what's going on. For years competitors failed to understand exactly what Google was doing.

Second, they are complex. Even with the fullest understanding, appropriating not one activity but several takes time and effort. Turning Dell into Apple would involve not only investment in hardware design, but also software development, relationships with third-party manufacturers, online content management, links to music and book publishers and building a dedicated community of obsessive consumer advocates. No small task!

Third, systems involve multiple trade-offs. It's a fair bet that traditional supermarkets won't copy Aldi's model. The average supermarket proposition typically demands multiple items per category. Stores are set up to handle complex cross-docking to and from multiple destinations, nothing ever runs out and pricing is controlled with military precision. The Aldi offering of narrow, predominantly private-label ranges involves too many sacrifices.

An understanding of activity systems explains in part why few strategists today cling to the old-fashioned belief that strategies should be locked away in secret. Most strategies do not rely upon a secret formula or a secret ingredient.

Even after Coca-Cola's famous formula leaked out,[9] no one succeeded in copying the company, and we suspect that they never will.

So far so good, but this all comes with some health warnings.

First, when executives indulge in commentary on "business strategy" it is frequently little more than pseudo-science with a very low burden of proof – or observations made with the supreme confidence of hindsight. It's easy to be wise after the event, but an acute ability to move quickly and decisively before things are well-understood can be one of the biggest sources of advantage.

Returning to the concept of "resource-based" sources of competitive advantage, Margaret Peteraf[10] has examined the conditions for this to become sustainable in detail. In particular, she splits "limits to competition" into two types which we find useful:

- *Ex Post limits to competition*, where an organisation can invest in (or buy into) an advantage before its value has been widely understood. She describes this as delivering "rents sustained" – where income continues to be generated long after everyone else can see what you are doing
- *Ex Ante limits to competition*, where the advantage is clear for all to see but you can somehow protect it. Activity systems are one such example. This by comparison is "rents not offset by costs" – where income generated far exceeds how much it costs you. This is the economists' idea of differentia-

---

9 You can make your own Coca-Cola from recipes in Pendergrast, M., 1993, *For God, Country, and Coca-Cola: The Definitive History of the Great American Soft Drink and the Company That Makes It.*
10 Peteraf, M., 1993, 'The Cornerstones of Competitive Advantage: A Resource-Based View', *Strategic Management Journal*, Vol. 14, pp. 179–191.

tion (charging more) that we will meet again in **Model 7.1 Porter's Generic Strategies**.

There is much in the body of knowledge about organisations that prioritise innovation and closeness to customers. Organisations that choose this as their direction need to work at it, since information doesn't flow freely, especially with regard to emerging opportunities and new technologies. It takes energy to move information around, to react to it and to gear an organisation around it.

Two relevant examples from within this book are **Model 3.3 Business Strategy Typology** and *Product Leadership* or *Customer Intimacy* within **Model 7.2 – The Discipline of Market Leaders**.

Figures 3.4
Sources of
Competitive
Advantage.

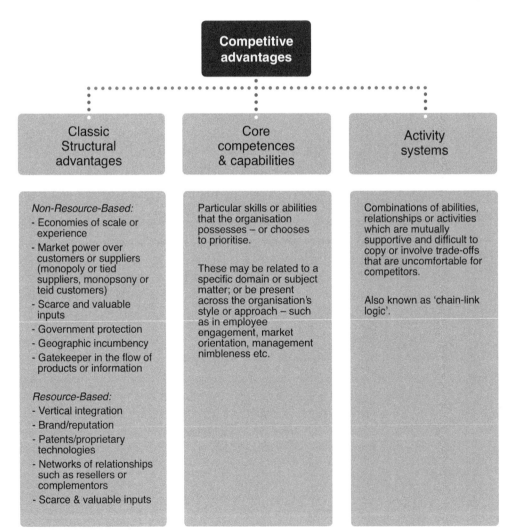

Competitive advantages		
Classic Structural advantages	**Core competences & capabilities**	**Activity systems**
Non-Resource-Based: - Economies of scale or experience - Market power over customers or suppliers (monopoly or tied suppliers, monopsony or teid customers) - Scarce and valuable inputs - Government protection - Geographic incumbency - Gatekeeper in the flow of products or information *Resource-Based:* - Vertical integration - Brand/reputation - Patents/proprietary technologies - Networks of relationships such as resellers or complementors - Scarce & valuable inputs	Particular skills or abilities that the organisation possesses – or chooses to prioritise. These may be related to a specific domain or subject matter; or be present across the organisation's style or approach – such as in employee engagement, market orientation, management nimbleness etc.	Combinations of abilities, relationships or activities which are mutually supportive and difficult to copy or involve trade-offs that are uncomfortable for competitors. Also known as 'chain-link logic'.

3.5 THREE HORIZONS OF GROWTH

Managers frequently feel that they are juggling the short-term and the long-term; the urgent and the important.

Baghai, Coley and White's concept *The Three Horizons of Growth*[11] gives us a mental model to deal with these tensions and think about how we might logically work out how to balance them.

While it is tempting to think of each horizon as a timeframe, in fact each is better defined in the context of product or business-unit maturity:

- Horizon one is about what the organisation is currently known for – its focus within the present mature state
- Horizon two is for new ventures (question marks or stars in the BCG Matrix, see **Model 1.4**)
- Horizon Three are very early-stage ideas and concepts – which may or may not go on to become future revenue generators.

Baghai, Coley and White's book *The Alchemy of Growth* is a useful reminder that we need to consider the short, medium and long-term if the organisation is to persist healthily, particularly within a rapidly changing environment. "How healthy are my horizons?" is one of the questions that they pose.

Before you race off and consider the exciting stuff in the distant future, however, the authors remind us that without surviving Horizon One, there will be no Horizon Two or Three. Their advice is: "Companies whose core businesses are under attack should be thinking above all about earning the right to grow. Before managers get carried away with new ideas, they must achieve solid performance in their core businesses".

Figure 3.5 summarises six key diagnoses based on performance in each of the horizons.

---

11 Baghai, M., Coley S., & White, D., 1999, *The Alchemy of Growth*, Orion Publishing, London.

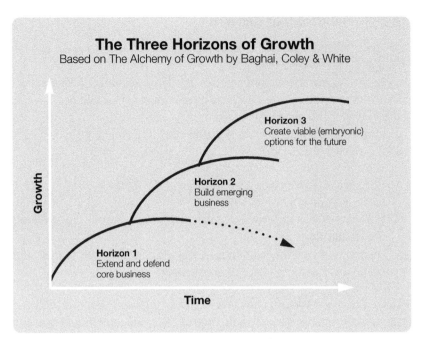

The Three Horizons of Growth
Based on The Alchemy of Growth by Baghai, Coley & White

Figure 3.5
Three Horizons of Growth. Adapted with permission from Baghai et al. (1999) © 1999, 2000 by McKinsey & Company, Inc., United States.

Diagnosis	HORIZON 1	HORIZON 2	HORIZON 3
'Under Siege'	✗	✗	✗
'Running out of steam'	✓	✗	✗
'Losing the right to grow'	✗	✓	✓
'Inventing a new future'	✗	✓✗	✓✗
'Generating ideas but not business'	✓	✗	✓
'Failing to seed for the future'	✓	✓	✗

3.6 SYNERGY ... OR NOT?

Few terms – except perhaps "disruption" – can challenge the word "synergy" for its position at the top of the business meeting bingo card. Variously used as a justification for investments, acquisitions, mergers or just plain product decisions; it's a classic example of unsubstantiated opinion, or in other words, irrefutable claptrap.

Shared know-how	Often this is tacit, rather than written down
Coordinated strategies	Joint responses, avoidance of internal competition
Shared tangible resources	Using the same physical assets or resources – avoiding duplicated effort
Vertical integration	Coordinating flow from one unit to another – improve efficiency & utilisation
Pooled negotiating power	Combined purchases
Combined business creation	Together, these businesses are greater than the sum of the parts

Figure 3.6
Potential Sources of Synergy. Reproduced with permission from Mishra, D. P., *Product Management* Lecture, Melbourne Business School 2008.

What is synergy anyway? Our diagram from Prof Debi Mishra in **Figure 3.6** summarises the main sources of value creation when two businesses or two products come together.

Synergy is seductive. But even where it does deliver benefits, it also brings opportunity costs and the net result is far from guaranteed to be positive. In their Harvard Business Review article, **Desperately Seeking Synergy**,[12] Michael Goold and Andrew Campbell explore this further. Four managerial biases which make chiefs overly keen to pursue synergy (or see synergy when in fact there is little) are:

1. Synergy bias
   - Management overestimates the benefits of synergy
   - They believe that synergy must be pursued – or is even *the* primary goal of senior management
   - They look for synergy opportunities everywhere
2. Parenting bias
   - Senior management need to entice divisional managers into cooperating because they assume senior managers are prejudiced against synergy
   - (In reality, it seems unlikely that managers would avoid synergy if it was valuable to them. There are usually good reasons for divisions choosing not to cooperate with a centralised command)
3. Skills bias
   - A belief that synergy can be achieved with the skills currently in the organisation

12 Goold, M., & Campbell, A., September–October 1998, 'Desperately Seeking Synergy', *Harvard Business Review*, Vol. 76, pp. 131–143.

- Assuming that the skills you have today will help you in the future
- An inability to recognise that self and colleagues lack required skills
4. Upside bias
    - Blinkered focus on the upsides without due consideration to the downsides of synergy
    - Example – an obsession with synergy may:
        - Reduce personal accountability
        - Impede or distract from organisational change
    - "Synergy's downsides are every bit as real as its upsides; they're just not seen as clearly"

Goold and Andrew Campbell suggest that in order to proceed with a synergy programme, managers should carefully undertake three steps.

1. Size the Prize
    - Clarify real objectives – avoid warm and fuzzy feel-good phrases
    - Avoid equivocation – be as precise as possible. It may help to define required capabilities; see **Model 3.1 Capabilities and Core Competences**.
    - Break down into components – establish rough benefit in each area
2. Pinpoint the Parenting/Partner Opportunity
    - Corporate executives should start with the assumption that when it makes good commercial sense, the business-unit managers will usually cooperate without the need for corporate involvement"
    - The parent's role may be best utilised as any of the following
        - Perception opportunities – showing where synergy can be beneficial
        - Evaluation opportunities – help with assessing costs and benefits
        - Motivation opportunities – incentives and encouragement
        - Implementation opportunities – resourcing and bringing the right skills on board
3. Bring downsides to light
    - To correct the inherent bias of synergy strategies, look for the downsides
    - Consider exploring synergy in a small way first

4   Analysis / Customers

Customers are the ultimate source of value.

Somebody, somewhere, must buy a product or a service to create a market and allow a business to exist. So, who are these people who buy or might buy your product? What motivates them to buy and how do they go about the task? This understanding should form the basis of every market-focused strategy, but it doesn't.

Products rarely fail because they don't work. They usually fail because they don't have a market willing to buy the product at the right price, at the right time and in sufficient numbers. A common mistake is to theorise in abstract how customers think and how they "will" behave, without actually bothering to check with them. Time spent here is well worth the investment – and the earlier the better.

Since we first started writing this compendium over a decade ago, there has been a lot of buzz about customers. It's almost as if an entire generation of consultants thought that they'd discovered customer-centricity and that by brandishing what they'd unearthed, they would be able to unlock unlimited value.

Two-sided markets have customers on both sides. Instead of a typical value chain where we add value to goods by processing, bundling or wholesaling them, this occurs where we create additional value upstream as well as downstream. This is particularly exciting and challenging depending upon your perspective. Of course, there is still a chain of information or a flow of goods or people, but in a very real sense, a two-sided platform creates value everywhere by treating both supply-side and demand-side users as customers.

When thinking about demand for your own products, try to be objective. In particular, be careful about projecting your own rationalisation onto real customers. If you're selling the product, you're probably biased. Chances are, no real customer thinks it's as good as you do.

DOI: 10.4324/9781003038276-4

WHAT TO LOOK OUT FOR

Don't delay getting in front of customers. For example, for an early-stage business or a new product, spending more time finessing marcoms than researching users is a common trap. On the other hand, it is possible to *over-research* customers. When you're getting nothing back that is new, or if you already knew this stuff, it's time to stop and deliver something.

A dangerous pitfall is to build a solution based on an untested assumption. Solving a problem that doesn't exist for your customers may result in a big problem for you instead!

A second pitfall is to underestimate how hard it is for customers to change from what they've always done. Even if there's evident logic in your new way of working, the switchover will incur a range of human and business costs.

A third pitfall is to think "build it and they will come". However good the product is, this statement is *never* true.

Finally, a comment about brands. A smart new logo on its own will achieve very little. In isolation, it's very unlikely to lead to increased brand equity, and if it tells a story that's inconsistent with the broader customer experience then it could backfire badly.

4.1 CORE, ACTUAL AND AUGMENTED PRODUCT

It was Theodore Levitt who famously observed in 1960 that "People don't want to buy a quarter-inch drill. They want a quarter-inch hole." The common sense of his insight is as fresh and relevant today as it was back then. Again, and again generations of companies get tripped up by what Levitt described as "Marketing Myopia":[1]

- Kodak thought it made film rather than pictures
- The early US railway operators thought they were in the business of trains rather than transport (some turned down a government offer to become involved in the nascent air cargo sector because they were "railway men")
- In the early 2000s, media companies were forced to understand they are in the business of content rather than broadcasting or printing. (Newspapers arguably contain little "news" and are rarely consumed on "paper")
- It's debatable whether Airbnb and Marriott are in the same category or not

Those who fall for the myopic trap become so focused on the product they are selling, rather than the customer need that it satisfies, they fail to respond when

---

1 Levitt, T., 1960, 'Marketing Myopia', *Harvard Business Review*, Vol. 38, pp. 45–56.

new and better solutions appear to address that same customer need.

In the years following Levitt, many commentators have picked up the theme. The notion of multiple tiers within the "total product" first appeared in Philip Kotler's book *Marketing Management*[2] of which there are more editions than we care to count.

Our diagram is a simplification of Kotler's. We believe that this should be the first and most fundamental model that most organisations should use to think about customers.

As an example, take the Australian flag-carrier Qantas. The core product for an airline is time-critical, long-distance travel. For business people it is the ability to be in another city for a short meeting; for holidaymakers, that they can spend more time at a distant holiday destination. The actual product is what is sold to facilitate this – booking services, baggage, aircraft seats, cabin service etc. The augmented product is that which is offered to enhance or differentiate the offering, such as complimentary drinks and meals. (Have you noticed how much of what was augmented product in airlines is now being charged for and as such has become actual product?) So, for an airline, potential competitive threats come from anything that can get our businessperson or holidaymaker to their chosen meeting or destination faster. Today that might be high-speed trains – tomorrow, who knows? Not just Hyperloops, Maglevs, and space travel? But also, as the Covid pandemic has shown us, Zoom, Webex, Around or Jitsi video conferencing.

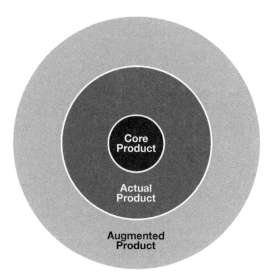

Figure 4.1
Tiers of Product.

There's a profound insight hidden in the Levitt quote that leads us to the "as-a-service" economy of today: *Why sell people a drill at all if it's the hole that they want?* A drill bit (or a car, or a lawnmower) is only active for a fraction of

---

2 Kotler, P., *Marketing Management*, various editions.

its life. Thanks to the web, it has become much easier to coordinate fractional or shared ownership of assets at scale – the move from ownership to usage models – something that few would have foreseen in the 1960s.

4.2 THE OPPORTUNITY EVALUATION MATRIX

In their book *Strategic Marketing Problems*, Kerin and Peterson set out their Opportunity Evaluation criteria.[3] They form a customer-centric matrix covering customer type, customer needs and mechanisms for satisfying those needs.[4] This has echoes of several other models in this section, notably **Model 4.5 The Job-to-Be-Done and Outcome-Driven Innovation**, which we'll meet next.

Figure 4.2
Opportunity Evaluation Matrix. Source: Roger A. Kerin and Robert A. Peterson, *Strategic Marketing Problems: Cases and Comments*, 12th ed (Pearson Education Inc., 2010) p. 66. Reprinted with the permission of the copyright holder, Roger A. Kerin.

MARKET NICHE CRITERION	CUSTOMER TYPE	CUSTOMER NEEDS	MEANS FOR SATISFYING CUSTOMER NEEDS
COMPETITIVE ACTIVITY	How many organisations are competing for each customer group? Who are they?	Which of the organisations are satisfying customer needs?	What strategies are being used to satisfy customer needs?
CUSTOMER REQUIREMENTS	What affects the customer's willingness and ability to buy?	What customer needs, if any, are not being satisfied?	Is the technology for satisfying customer needs changing?
DEMAND AND SUPPLY	Do different customers types have different demand levels? If so, what are they?	Do we have or can we acquire resources to satisfy customer needs?	Is the demand for the means for satisfying customer needs changing?
PESTLE FORCES	How sensitive are different customer types to these forces?	How sensitive are customer needs to these forces?	How sensitive are the means for satisfying customer needs to these forces?
ORGANISATIONAL CAPABILITIES	Can we a) Gain access to and b) Supply these customers?	Which customer needs can our organisation satisfy?	Do we have the financial, human, techologoical and marketing expertise to satisfy customer needs?

---

3 Kerin, R. A., & Peterson, R. A., 1998, *Strategic Marketing Problems: Case and Commands*, Prentice Hall, Upper Saddle River.

4 The representation shown here incorporates suggestions from Prof Susan Ellis.

The PESTLE forces in the diagram refer to the Political, Economic, Scientific, Technological, Legal and Environmental of **Model 5.1**.

4.3 VALUE PROPOSITIONS

The term "Value Proposition" has gained renewed currency in recent years, in particular, because of its inclusion in much of the commentary around **Model 8.6 Business Model Canvas** and associated literature about start-ups. It also pops up in the chatter that accompanies the current phrases du jour *Human-Centred Design* and *Design Thinking.*

The term is not new.

You could almost be mistaken for thinking that value propositions *only* mattered for early-stage businesses, but in fact nothing could be further from the truth.

According to the *Value Proposition Design*[5] (a spin-off book from the excellent *Business Model Canvas*), value propositions can be couched in terms of

- Gains created
- Pains relieved (including risks reduced)
- The particular products and services that achieve the above

Apart from the fact that gains created and pains relieved can sometimes overlap, this is an eminently sensible way of looking at the world.

In fact, this is the old idea of "benefits versus features" recycled – as we shall see in **Model 4.1 Core, Actual and Augmented Product**. It also closely links to Christensen's Job-to-Be-Done and Ulwick's Outcome-Driven Innovation (**Model 4.5**), since the only way to make sense of making gains or fixing pains is to know what issues the customer needs to address in the first place.

Solving problems is always particularly attractive when pitching your idea. Indeed, many are the businesses that have crashed and burned in the face of promising cash projections fixing a "problem" worth many millions of dollars. During the dot-com boom of the early 2000s, companies like Pets.com and Lastminute.com claimed that they were fixing widespread problems. Some were; others were not.

It may be stating the obvious, but when it comes to solving problems for customers, what matters is how painful the problem is. Any management team will have a long list of problems that they could fix – but they are only likely to fix the most painful and, probably, the most immediate. Whether you can build a cost benefit analysis that is mathematically worthwhile is irrelevant. There's

5 Osterwalder, A. et al., 2014, *Value Proposition Design: How to Create Products and Services Customers Want,* Wiley, Hoboken.

an old adage about whether your product or service is providing a "vitamin or a painkiller"[6] which is a sobering reminder of this.

We'll return to value propositions again in **Model 7.2 The Discipline of Market Leaders**.

4.4 VALUE PROPOSITIONS FOR B2B

In the specific case of B2B markets, the paper *Customer Value Propositions in Business Markets*, Anderson, Narus and Van Rossum (again, Harvard Business Review) is incisive.[7]

The paper suggests there are three types of value propositions all of which aim to encourage customers to see the financial benefits of your product. These are

- **All benefits** regardless of competitors
- **All Favourable Points of Difference** versus competitors
- **Resonating Focus** – a select few points of great importance to customers

Furthermore, managers should pay particular attention to the potential pitfalls:

- Benefit assertion – mistakenly assumes that all benefits are automatically differences. In fact, many benefits are points of parity and thus not reasons to switch
- Value Presumption – mistakenly assumes that a favourable difference is automatically valuable. Of course, there will be differences, the trick is to identify the valuable ones.

Resonating Focus introduces the idea that you should consider both points of difference *and* parity. When structuring your value proposition, it may be prudent to include *some* points where you *differ* from competitors and *some* where you *match* them – for instance, if you offer some fancy benefits but *also* deliver on the basics at the same level as your competitors.

Last, it's important to demonstrate customer value – and to document it. Typically for business customers, this takes the form of a cost benefit analysis: you'll spend n, but you'll save x and generate y as a consequence. Beware: a positive cost benefit analysis does not mean that customers will come running!

---

6 This metaphor has been around for a while. See for example Deeb, G., July 2014, 'Is Your Startup Building a 'Vitamin' or a 'Painkiller'?, *Forbes*.

7 Anderson, J. C., Narus, J. A., & Van Rossum, W., 2006, 'Customer Value Propositions in Business Markets', *Harvard Business Review*, Vol. 84, pp. 91–99.

VALUE PROPOSITION:	ALL BENEFITS	FAVORABLE POINTS OF DIFFERENCE	RESONATING FOCUS
Consists of:	All benefits customers receivefrom a market offering	All favorable points of difference a market offering has relative to the next best alternative	The one or two points of difference (and, perhaps, a point of parity) whose improvement will deliver the greatest value to the customer for the foreseeable future
Answers the customer question:	"Why should our firm purchase your offering?"	"Why should our firm purchase your offering instead of your competitor's?"	"What is *most* worthwhile for our firm to keep in mind about your offering?"
Requires:	Knowledge ofown market offering	Knowledge of own market offering and next best alternative	Knowledge of how own market offering delivers superior value to customers, compared with next best alternative
Has the potential pitfall:	Benefit assertion	Value presumption	Requires customer value research

Figure 4.3
Value Propositions
andTheir Pitfalls.
Reprinted with
permission of
Harvard Business
Publishing
from Anderson
et al. (2006).
Copyright ©2006
Harvard Business
Publishing; all rights
reserved.

4.5 THE JOB-TO-BE-DONE AND OUTCOME-DRIVEN INNOVATION

In recent years there's been growing popularity in talking about "problems" and "tasks" as things that organisations should focus on.

Clayton Christensen popularised his portmanteau "job-to-be-done" in the early 2000s.[8] Those eagle-eyed amongst you will recognise that this is again the *Why before What* that we met at the start of this book with Collins, Rumelt (and yes, even Simon Sinek).

But as with many of the concepts in this book, it has much earlier roots. For example, in their review of the "House of Quality" concept, John Hauser and Don Clausing outlined a similar structure.[9] In their version – which is more product-centric rather than customer-centric – a feature is broken down into attributes that give rise to a particular outcome.

Christensen tells us "People don't simply buy products or services, they "hire" them to make progress in specific circumstances". From this seemingly mundane insight flows quite a lot of consequence. Products do things for their customers; they do this in a context – a time and a place; and they compete against other alternatives to do the same job.

---

8 Christensen, C. et al., September 1016, 'Know Your Customers' "Jobs to Be Done"', *Harvard Business Review*, Vol. 94, No. 9, pp. 54–62.

9 Hauser, J., & Clausing, D., May 1988, 'The House of Quality', *Harvard Business Review*, Vol. 3, pp. 63–73.

It helps when thinking about the job-to-be-done to dig in a little too: Be aware that people may misreport what job they are doing. When someone thumbs through Facebook, are they really connecting with friends, or are they looking to fill in downtime? This is the core, actual, augmented product that we met in **Model 4.1**.

Anthony Ulwick builds more structure into Christensen's work by suggesting that each task or "job-to-be-done" can be further subdivided into "metrics" or "outcomes". You can think of a task or job as something that a customer might say in answer to the question "what are you trying to do here?"; while the outcomes break this down further. There will be more from Ulwick in the next model.

Ulwick suggests that when looking to define these outcomes we should consider phrases beginning with words like *maximise*, *minimise*, *increase*, *reduce* and so on. The company and its competitors can be scored quantitatively on each of these metrics. Note also how this is starting to sound like specific, measurable, achievable, relevant, time-bound (SMART) goals or objectives and key results (OKRs) – see **Model 8.3** – but through a deeply customer-centric lens.

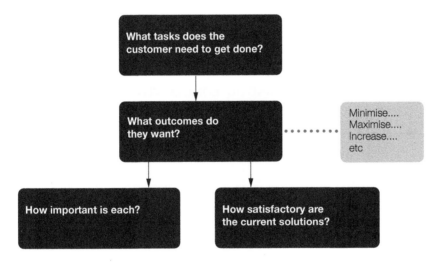

Figure 4.4
From Jobs to Outcomes. This Image Builds Upon the Ideas Expressed in Ulwick, A., *What Customers Want.*

4.6 IMPORTANCE X SATISFACTION ANALYSIS

This seemingly simple idea was first popularised by Anthony Ulwick in his book *Outcome-Driven Innovation*[10] and then picked up by Dan Olsen in *The Lean Product Playbook.*[11] Ask your customers not only what's important to them but where the gaps are – in the products they use already.

Importance x satisfaction analysis appears staggeringly obvious as soon as you see it – but it's easy to forget, which is why we include it here.

10 Ulwick, A., *What Customers Want.*
11 Olsen, D., *The Lean Product Playbook.*

The idea is that for all of the tasks or outcomes that a customer needs to get done, importance alone is necessary but not sufficient for it to be worth a company investing in serving.

In considering whether a feature – or whole product – is worth pursuing, there are two potential pitfalls for product-market fit. One of these is that the problem isn't worth fixing; the other is that it is already adequately served. In other words, a high level of importance is **necessary but not sufficient** for the business to pursue it.

You can identify where to focus your efforts by looking for problems that are *both* seriously important *and* poorly addressed by existing products or services.

It's important to note that there is yet a third filter to consider – does our business possess the right complementary assets, access or positioning in order to provide the services identified by this model? Put another way, *why are we the right people to solve this problem for these customers?* Do we have the right in the eyes of customers to present ourselves in this way?

Figure 4.5 shows how an importance x satisfaction chart can help the business in the process of prioritisation. Ulwick proposes a scatter plot like this can be split into three segments: over-served, appropriately served and under-served.

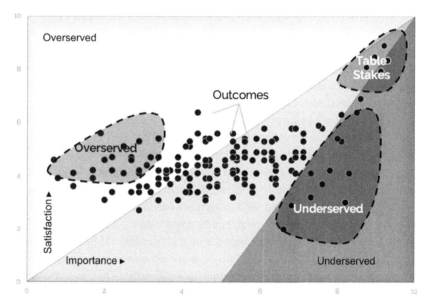

Figure 4.5
Importance x Satisfaction Analysis. Image reproduced with permission from Strategyn Based on Concepts Outlined in Ulwick, A., *What Customers Want*.

There's another connection to Christensen here. Over-served is precisely the same area that we will meet in the Performance Trajectory of Disruptive Innovation (those interested in learning more can now jump ahead to **Model 7.5 Disruptive Innovation**). This connection also reminds us that the market is far from static. Today's area of opportunity may be addressed by another player tomorrow. Similarly, today's appropriately served task may be considered under-served by the time you next survey the market.

4.7 SOURCES OF BRAND EQUITY

So, you think you've got a great brand or perhaps you would like to build one? You need to know about brand equity. As we saw in **Model 1.6 Brand Charter and Desired Reputation**, today brands are generally regarded based on reputation or desired reputation.[12] In many organisations they are the firm's most valuable assets with a direct impact on revenue, margin and profit.

Kevin Keller made a great contribution to the discussion on brand through his use of the term "brand equity" and his definition: "A brand has positive customer-based brand equity when consumers react more favorably to a product and the way it is marketed when the brand is identified than when it is not".[13] Before Keller, Jerome McCarthy talked about "brand familiarity"[14] which, it turns out, is a very similar idea.

Under Keller's definition, brand equity relates to how consumers behave in response to the brand. In line with the widely accepted understanding of the link between cognition and action, brand equity is assumed to be the result of brand knowledge. This in turn is driven by awareness (recall and recognition) and image (based on associations). The diagram in **Figure 4.6** – which is based on Keller's – shows how this breaks down further.

A brand with strong brand equity will deliver benefits like reduced price sensitivity and greater customer retention. But as noted in Keller's definition, brand equity will also lead to increased effectiveness of marketing activity since the presence of the brand will ensure a higher cut through. In this way, the concept of brand equity relates to the broader idea of gaining benefits from particular resources or assets as we shall see in **Model 3.4 Sources of Competitive Advantage**.

A lot of time has been wasted looking for a single measure of brand equity – *imagine if it were possible to assess each brand with a single, cross-category score and say that one has more of this special quality than another!* Sadly, attempts to find the one objective measurement are doomed to failure. Aaker summed up the challenge thus: "[Measuring brand equity] can require dozens of measures. Although each potentially has diagnostic value, the use of so many measures is unwieldy. For reporting and tracking purposes it would be useful and convenient to have a single summary measure…".[15] But setting aside the wishful thinking, Aaker notes that there are difficulties not only in calibrating the various measures but in determining what weights to place on them.

---

12 Contrast the noun "brand" which generally refers to a combination of promise and reputation with the verb "branding" which generally has retained more of its historical meaning. Branding generally refers to the act of applying logo and/or graphic design to visual, and sometimes audio, communications.

13 Keller, K. L., January 1993, 'Conceptualizing, Measuring, and Managing Customer-Based Brand Equity', *Journal of Marketing*, Vol. 57, No. 1, pp. 1–22.

14 McCarthy, J. E., *Basic Marketing*, various editions from 1960 onwards.

15 Aaker, D., 1996, *Building Strong Brands*, Free Press, New York.

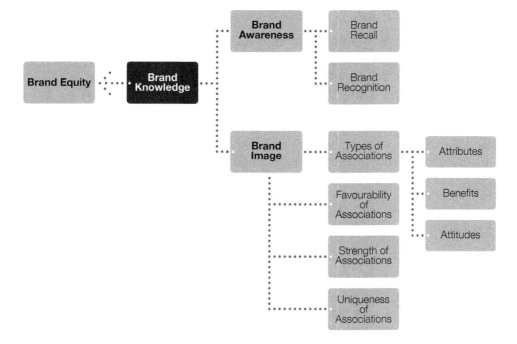

Figure 4.6
Keller's Drivers
of Brand Equity.
Republished with
permission of
Sage Publications
Inc., from
Keller (1993);
permission
conveyed through
Copyright
Clearance Center,
Inc.

Even though brand equity can't be easily measured in a single metric, it is very important. But it isn't the only "intangible asset" that a company can possess though – we'll cover the others in **Model 4.21 Market-Based Assets**.

A few words of warning:

Sometimes managers seeking great brand equity (and let's face it, who wouldn't) decide that what they need is a smart new logo and some advertising.[16] Of course this can help, but it is far from the best way to build a brand. Even a well-defined image does not automatically translate into brand equity. Consider this:

- A smart logo will do nothing for your brand if no one sees it.
- A great advertising campaign will do even less if your business has a reputation for poor quality or shoddy service.
- A great set of associations (such as being known for luxury, or careful, considered or safe) will do nothing for your business if they have no relevance to the category in which you seek to operate.

Brand equity may be notoriously difficult to define but it's relatively simple compared to *brand value* – which is a minefield of controversy and confusion. *Brand value* tries to ascribe a financial value to a brand which is always contentious (who decides?) and frequently mixed up in the perspective of an acquirer – as Raggio and Leone have pointed out in their excellent review of the topic.[17] We suggest sticking with brand equity instead.

---

16 This section draws on Grannell, C., 2009, 'Untangling Brand Equity, Value and Health', originally published by *brandchannel.com* and republished by *brandvas.io*.

17 Raggio, R., & Leone, B., 2009, 'Chasing Brand Value', *Journal of Brand Management*, Vol. 16, No. 4, pp. 248–263.

4.8 BRAND HEALTH: BAV

Although there's no single measure of brand equity or value, there are several ways of considering the health of a brand.

In our opinion, two of the best are called BrandZ and Brand Asset Valuator (BAV). Strictly speaking, both are resources – giant databases of comparative information – and so don't quite meet the "tools" criteria for inclusion in this book. However, each depends upon useful constructs that can help you think about brands, even without the performance data.

BAV[18] looks at brands as part of the culture so provides a cross-category perspective. It assesses 60,000 brands on four criteria, called "pillars":

- Differentiation – uniqueness or distinctiveness
- Relevance – appropriateness to the customer or their needs
- Esteem – perception of quality and respect
- Knowledge – how well recognised and understood

The BAV model has its roots in academia and it's no surprise that these criteria echo the sources of brand equity proposed by Keller in **Model 4.7 Sources of Brand Equity**. BAV then rolls the four pillars into two simple measures: Differentiation and relevance collectively become **Brand Strength**, whilst esteem and knowledge make up **Brand Stature**. It is the latter that indicates future growth potential.

Iconic brands score well on all characteristics, and those with universally low scores tend to be newcomers or going nowhere. It's when the scores differ that things get interesting.

- Brands with high differentiation and relevance but low esteem and knowledge may present untapped opportunities
- Brands where low differentiation and relevance are accompanied by high awareness and esteem are likely to fall on tough times – if they haven't already

Any brand owner should have (at the very least), a gut sense of where their product sits on these dimensions, and in which way it is heading. Just do yourself a favour and resist the temptation to overstate the value or importance of your brand. We also saw this health warning in **Model 3.1 Capabilities and Core Competences**.

The analysis of Netflix and Blockbuster in **Figure 4.8** shows two common paths that brands follow. Two brands in the same market peaked at a similar point – high stature and high esteem – but Netflix ten years earlier was a niche brand and it took Blockbuster about the same timeframe to become a classic case of brand fatigue – a familiar icon with low relevance.

---

18 BAV and Brand Asset Valuator is © BAV Group. www.bavgroup.com.

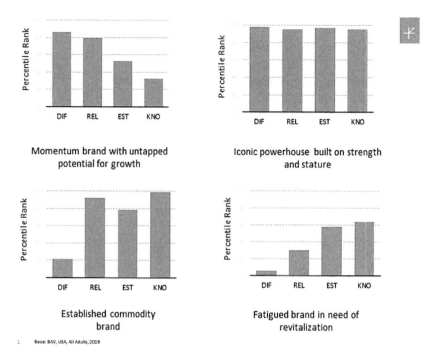

Figure 4.7

BAV Archetypes. Reprinted with permission from BAV Group.

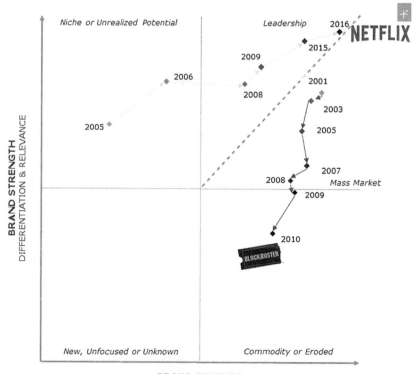

BRAND STATURE
ESTEEM & KNOWLEDGE

Figure 4.8

BAV Comparison of Netflix and Blockbuster. Research Based on US Adults. Reprinted with permission from BAV Group.

4.9 BRAND HEALTH: BRANDZ

BrandZ[TM][19] considers the strength of the relationship that a brand has with the population. It draws on several concepts including some aspects of the marketing hierarchy of effects, which we will meet in **Model 4.17 Buyer Readiness and the Purchase Funnel**, and the drivers of brand knowledge from **Model 4.7 Sources of Brand Equity**.

BrandZ scores brands within their category. For example, you can compare different brands of beer or smart speakers or pet food. **Figure 4.9** shows a comparison of UK grocery brands.

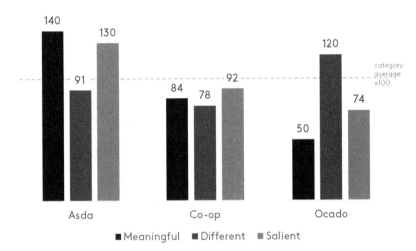

Comparison of three competing grocery brands in the UK
– brand equity components indexed on category average (=100)

Figure 4.9
BrandZ Analysis of Three Major UK Grocery Brands. Reprinted with permission from Kantar.

The tool also assesses brands on many other characteristics including trust and advocacy. The key insight is that wider brand associations can give us an indication of the potential of the brand to grow and deliver value in future. Simply being famous alone won't cut it.

BrandZ reminds us of the old adage that to be valuable, a difference must be meaningful. We'll return to this in **Model 4.4 Value Propositions for B2B**.

Well-known brands that do a poor job of utilising their awareness will likely score low on purpose, present uninspiring communications, offer an irrelevant brand experience and, as a consequence, have a low level of audience

---

19 BrandZ[TM] is © Kantar. www.kantar.com/brandz.

engagement. It's no surprise then that such a brand will lack advocacy, even if there is some residual trust in the brand.

Research by BrandZ[20] shows how difference, and to a lesser extent, meaning in the eyes of consumers contribute to the valuation of the companies that own them. **Figure 4.10** shows the difference in average global index score for brands that grew their brand value the most when compared with those that declined or grew least, from 2020 to 2021. Interestingly, it shows that salience (being easy to recall) is negatively correlated to growth.

Figure 4.10
Impact of Meaningful and Different on Growing Brands According to BrandZ. Reprinted with permission from Kantar.

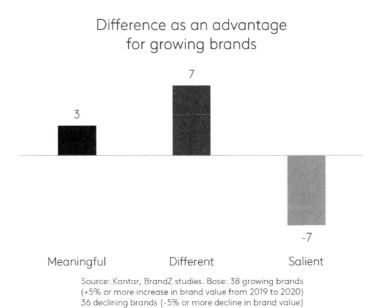

Difference as an advantage for growing brands

Source: Kantar, BrandZ studies. Base: 38 growing brands
(+5% or more increase in brand value from 2019 to 2020)
36 declining brands (-5% or more decline in brand value)

We've included both BAV and BrandZ in this book because both of the frameworks can be useful in thinking about any brand and its competitors. BAV and BrandZ databases can be used to track popular brands across multiple countries and compare them to competitors and category benchmarks. Today, analysis from both BrandZ and BAV is available commercially. Both publish reports of high-performing brands, and BrandZ also tracks the stock performance of a "Strong Brands Portfolio".

Curiously enough, the two tools are distant cousins. BAV was developed by Y&R in 1993. BrandZ was developed in 1998 by WPP, which later went on to acquire Y&R. BrandZ is now operated solely by market research consultancy Kantar.

---

20 Kyriakidi, M., 2021, *Why and How Should You Measure Brand Equity?* Kantar.com. https://www. kantar.com/inspiration/brands/why-and-how-should-you-measure-brand-equity.

4.10 RFM (RECENCY, FREQUENCY, MONETARY VALUE) ANALYSIS

RFM is a set of related concepts from what used to be called "Internet market-ing" but what is now firmly part of mainstream business.

In the days before subscription became the popular revenue model that it is today, revenue was typically not an annuity but a lumpy on-and-off flow of pay-ments from a variety of customers moving in and out of different purchase patterns.

In this environment it was – and still is – important to understand how differ-ent customers consume your products and use your services. Even businesses with subscription elements will generally have transactions over and above the predictable annuity of monthly payments.

The key ideas are:

- **Cohort Analysis** – you can group each successive wave of users, particularly of a web-based product, into cohorts. Unlike *segments* that are profiled by behav-iour or psychology, cohorts are defined by customers when they first started to interact with the business. Cohorts are sometimes used by epidemiologists to refer to successive waves of a virus – this serves as a good metaphor.

Cohorts are important because managers frequently tinker with what a business is offering – new or deprecated features, changes to bundles, or updated prices. An early cohort and a later cohort may look in many respects identical, but they will have experienced different messaging, they may be using different versions of a product; and they might be on different pricing plans. Because of the passage of time, they are by definition at different stages in the customer lifecycle (see **Model 4.18 The Adoption Curve**). If we assign customers who first transacted in 2020 as cohort 1 and customers who joined in 2021 as cohort 2, and we have a churn of 50%, then we would expect half of the first cohort to be giving up on the product as the second cohort is still having its first experience of the organisation.

- **Recency and Frequency** – now that cohorts are clear, this part is fairly obvi-ous. When did they last buy and at what rate are they coming back? The "monetary" part is how much they spent.
- **Propensity** – is a forward-looking view on how likely a customer is to buy. It may be based on recency and frequency, but once these patterns are understood, the likelihood of other customers spending *before they actually do so* is something that we can start to understand.

Another take on RFM is **loyalty-based segmentation**, where behaviour is used to create segments.

4.11 CUSTOMER LIFETIME VALUE (CLV)

We could have written another book just on customer metrics (and many people already have), but some key concepts deserve review here.

Customer Lifetime Value is, put simply, the Annual Recurring Revenue (ARR) of a customer multiplied by the typical Customer Lifetime.

$$CLV = ARR * CL$$

Customer Lifetime is just *one divided by the churn rate*, which is the proportion of customers that leave your business each year. Churn is typically expressed as a percentage.

$$CV = 1/Churn$$

In this sense, "value" is a bit of a misnomer, since true value is value to the bottom line – that is, profitability – yet in this case, it more commonly refers to the top line: sales. Far be it for us to challenge established conventions though, so there it is.

One way to think about this – particularly popular amongst early-stage businesses – is to compare CLV with Cost to Acquire (CTA)

$$CLV - CTA > 0$$

The simplest kind of ARR to understand is a subscription – hence the popularity of subscription-based pricing models in recent years. But transactional businesses can also use this type of analysis if their revenue is regular and predictable: for example, an accountant with a book of clients paying a fee each year for help with their tax return.

When you look at it like this, it's easy to see why subscription models have become so popular. First, the maths is easier; and second, they *seem* on the surface to be more predictable.

Recent economic shocks such as the global financial crisis and the Covid-19 pandemic have also demonstrated the appeal of recurring revenue from subscriptions, which are widely considered to be more stable. Then again, when someone cancels a subscription you face the challenge of having to win them back.

4.12 POCKET PRICING MODEL (PPM)

Way before pricing was seen as a business function, organisations would focus on achieving profitability from reducing average costs (productivity) or from selling more (volume). Historically, the price was a function of *cost plus a margin*. In fact, in many industrial sectors margin is still either explicitly or implicitly acknowledged as a price calculation – frequently being published or openly discussed in tenders.

Then came technology and scale. And the principle of zero marginal cost – something which to economists was a mere theoretical construct until relatively recently.

Fast forward to 2020 and the relationship between price and cost is well and truly broken. Many companies have a pricing function, or pricing as a formal part of finance, sales or product functions.

Back in 1992, when Michael Marn and Robert Rosiello published *Managing Price, Gaining Profit* in the Harvard Business Review,[21] these ideas were still in their infancy. Marn and Rosiello quantified it thus: "for a company with average economics, improving unit volume by 1% yields a 3.3% in operating profit … but … a 1% improvement in price, assuming no loss of volume, increases operating profit by 11.1%". (There's a heroic assumption in here, but we'll let that go for now, especially since even if volume does decline, you might still be better off.)

What makes this a truly seminal paper is the introduction of the PPM. The PPM is so-named not because it is a "pocket model" but because it refers to the "pocket price" – the actual contribution of a sale after discounting.

Most of us are familiar with invoiced prices being less than the prices on the rate card or catalogue – the list price. But customers frequently receive further discounts after the invoice has been raised such as discounts for quick payment. To get a true picture of the net figure paid by the customer consider other costs which may be absorbed (for example, freight), other expenses covered (a common one is advertising funding by the supplier), or margin reductions on other purchases (discounts elsewhere). Not to mention corporate hospitality.

These are tricks that every sales team knows – but frequently they are opaque to those running the organisation. As Marn and Rosiello put it, "many companies fail to manage the full range of components that contribute to the final transaction price".

Figure 4.11
The Pocket Price Waterfall. Reprinted with permission of Harvard Business Publishing from Marn and Rosiello (1992). Copyright ©1992 Harvard Business Publishing; all rights reserved.

Exhibit 2. In the Pocket Price Waterfall, each Element Represents a Revenue Leak

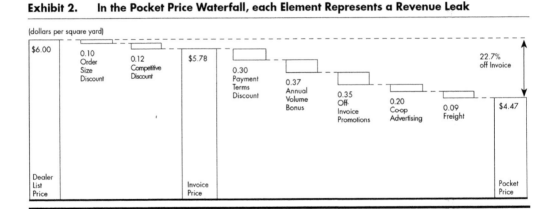

The diagram encourages us to consider the various ways in which the list price, and then the invoice price, are slashed. The waterfall looks different for every company, but the authors cite anonymous examples of revenue leakage of up to 23%.

More worryingly still, many firms will have a range of different pocket prices across their client base. Marn and Rosiello say they've witnessed huge variance between highest and lowest pocket prices within a single company – in many

---

21 Marn, M., & Rosiello, R., September–October 1992, 'Managing Price, Gaining Profit', *Harvard Business Review*, Vol. 70, No. 5, pp. 84–94.

cases over 100%. This means that some customers are paying twice as much as their peers for the same product or service.

No one is suggesting that there should be no discounts or rewards for good customers – just that there should be some governance rather than the nod and wink that keeps friends on side, and helps salespeople to avoid having difficult conversations.

Common sense, perhaps, but easier said than done.

A good tip from Marn and Rosiello is to start by looking at the outliers in the Pocket Price band. The top and bottom 10%–20% of transactions or customers are those to investigate – and "exception" or "outlier" report. Do volumes justify these deals? If not, they should stop.

4.13 THE PRICING SENSITIVITY METER (PSM) 1976

Price Sensitivity is a relative affair. It tends to be greater in high-cost categories (10% extra on a car is more than 10% on a bottle of ketchup) and the presence of competitors and low switching costs increases it. So much for the theory. But how do you work out what it actually is? The PSM Meter can help here.

Like many of the models that we feature, this has been renamed and repackaged more times than we care to imagine. The idea is to use market research to suggest a price range for your product before you've launched it.

To use the PSM model, a description of the product – or better still, a prototype – is accompanied by a short questionnaire or interview centred around just three or four questions.

Originally proposed (and named) by Peter Van Westendorp[22] in 1976, it has become a standard feature in much research ever since. Van Westendorp's original question set is as follows:

- At what price would you consider the product to be so expensive that you would not consider buying it? (Too expensive)
- At what price would you consider the product to be priced so low that you would feel the quality couldn't be very good? (Too cheap)
- At what price would you consider the product starting to get expensive, so that it is not out of the question, but you would have to give some thought to buying it? (Expensive)
- At what price would you consider the product to be a bargain – a great buy for the money? (Cheap)

At its simplest, the frequency of answers to the questions can provide us with a line graph that provides us with an understanding of how customers may react to pricing. But Van Westendorp takes it further.

The critical insight of the model is that the second pair of questions – "cheap" and "expensive" – both have an implied inverse. In other words, if

---

22 Van Westendorp, P., 1976, 'NSS-Price Sensitivity Meter (PSM) – A New Approach to Study Consumer Perception of Price', *Proceedings of the ESOMAR Congress.*

10% of respondents think that $100 is expensive for your new widget, then 90% of them should think that it is not expensive, even if they would never articulate it this way.

The acceptable price range falls between two points on a chart. By identifying where "Not Cheap" (the inverse of the "Cheap" question that you asked) overlaps with Too Cheap, you can consider this as the lowest price you would charge. Conversely, where "Not Expensive" (the inverse of "Expensive") crosses with "Too Expensive" this provides you with an upper boundary on pricing.

The Optimal Price Point (OPP) is where Too Expensive and Too Cheap intersect.

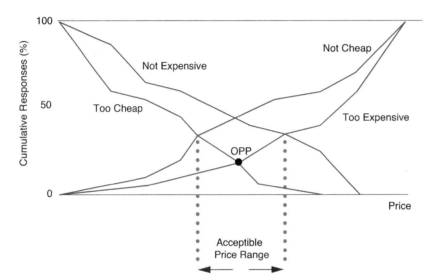

Figure 4.12
Pricing Sensitivity Meter Used to Analyse Pricing of a Product.

In this version of the PSM, it is critical that scores are plotted cumulatively – that is, each score is added to the scores for the prices below it – so that each line only curves in one direction. This is so that intersection points can be read off the graph.

The graph plots the cumulative results at each price point – so in a survey of 200 potential customers if $100 is reported by one respondent as "Too Expensive" and $80 by two respondents as "Too Expensive", these would be plotted as 1 and 3, respectively.

As per this diagram, you don't need to chart "Expensive" and "Cheap" as their purpose is just to generate the "Not Expensive" and "Not Cheap" lines.

Note that traditional economists tend to prefer the term "elasticity" instead of "sensitivity". The two relate to the same concept, but sensitivity is a much more flexible idea; whilst elasticity has a very strict meaning which we will meet in **Model 4.20 Demand Elasticity**.

The PSM can be used within different segments or to compare acceptable trigger points between non-customers and customers.

4.14 THE PRICING SENSITIVITY METER REDUX

A simplified version of the PSM features in *Monetizing Innovation* by Madhavan Ramanujam and Georg Tacke.[23] They propose three simple questions:

- What do you think is an acceptable price?
- What do you think is an expensive price?
- What is a prohibitively expensive price?

Ramanujam and Tacke recommend open-ended questions and envisage them as part of a face-to-face interview (what they call, ominously, "a deep willingness to pay discussion"), but we have used multiple-choice questions too. Asking the three questions with a dropdown list of prices simplifies charting the results.

To the best of our knowledge, it has never been proven that the sequencing of the questions affects the results, nor does it matter whether you give respondents prices to choose from or whether they pick their own prices.

Answers to the "acceptable price" question can then be plotted on a simple chart showing the *percentage of customers who find the price acceptable*. Unlike before, there is no need to create cumulative scores, as percentages can just be read off the chart.

Although not strictly a model of demand elasticity (see **Model 4.20**), it does visualise the intuition that for a range of prices there will usually be some proportion of customers who find a particular price acceptable. But just because seven out of ten respondents tell you that $99 is an acceptable price point, this does not mean that 70% will buy. As Van Westerndorp himself said, "price consciousness of this nature should never be equated with propensity to buy"[24] – which works both ways; customers might buy things they regard as expensive, and not buy things they claim are acceptably priced.

A further variation proposed by Jon Manning[25] is to incorporate the "expensive" and "prohibitively expensive" counts in a "Net Acceptable Price". The Net Acceptable Price for each price point is found by subtracting those who found a price expensive or prohibitively expensive from those who found the price acceptable.

There are many practical challenges facing both versions of the PSM. Do you have the data? And do you have the time? Waiting 12 months or more to see the impact on revenue is impractical in many circumstances.

Figure 4.13 shows the simplified three-question version of the PSM. In this example, none of the scores are cumulative which is why they move up and down. The plot in **Figure 4.14** is easier to read. The price becomes unacceptable just before reaching $200.

23 Ramanujam, M., & Tacke, G., 2016, *Monetizing Innovation*, John Wiley & Sons, Hoboken.

24 Van Westerndorp, P., 1976, 'NSS-Price Sensitivity Meter (PSM) - A New Approach to Study Consumer Perception of Price', *Proceedings of the ESOMAR Congress.*

25 Manning, J., 2021, *Overcoming Floccinaucinihilipilification: Valuing and Monetizing Products and Services.*

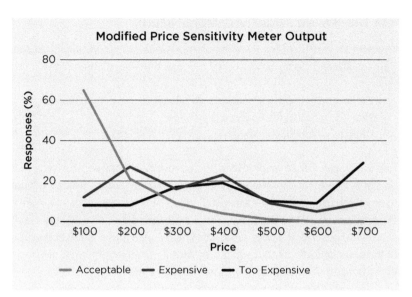

Figure 4.13
Three-Question
PSM. Reproduced
with permission
from Manning
(2021).

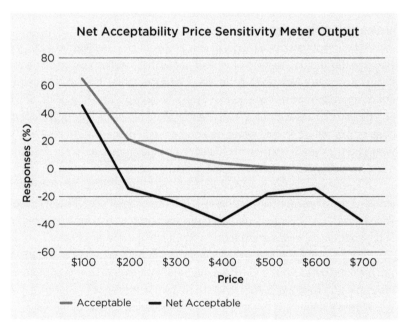

Figure 4.14
Adapted PSM
showing %
Acceptable and %
Net Acceptable.
Reproduced with
permission from
Manning (2021).

A more hands-on alternative to the PSM is to run an A/B test. Often touted as a holy grail in product testing it is notoriously difficult where pricing research is concerned because of the challenges in isolating users (so they don't talk to each other), sourcing a large enough sample, and ensuring equivalence between them. If you don't have time or resources to present identical products in identical separate markets, then one or the other version of the PSM is probably the way to go.

4.15 THE LONG TAIL

Ever heard the term "80-20 rule"? If you've had a job almost anywhere over the past few decades, you cannot fail to have come across it.

At its core is the idea that most of your profit/hassle/noise/clicks/clients/ complaints/praise comes from a small proportion of your accounts/customers/ pages/calls. And the portion that makes all of the noise is generally less than a quarter of the total.

OK. So what?

It turns out you can write a book about the implications of this apparently inane observation. And that book – *The Long Tail* by Chris Anderson[26] – is surprisingly thought-provoking.

Doing just about everything in the physical world carries a cost of some kind. A variable cost and often a fixed cost too – some pain or investment associated with tooling or setup of a new product, new production line or new colour of paint. Classical economics used to say that if you're only going to sell a small amount of your obscure kooky product variant, then *it just isn't worth doing*. In economics, we meet the concept of *minimum efficient scale* on the cost curve where the minimum cost has been achieved. We'll return to this in **Model 5.2 The Experience Curve**.

Anderson's hypothesis is that thanks to the Internet, things which were previously uneconomic are now worth doing; suggesting that this heralds a world with "unlimited choice". In a web-enabled world, marginal costs – for example, of maintaining a huge inventory of stock-keeping units that rarely sell – are minimal.

Incidentally, some of this was foreseen by Michael Porter a decade earlier when he wrote the seminal paper *Strategy and the Internet*;[27] a paper which considers how the Internet (and more specifically the web and web applications) influences industry structure: rivalry, substitutes, buyers, barriers to entry and suppliers.

In retail, we hear talk of the so-called "infinite aisle": the concept that stems from the removal of warehousing, stocking or working capital costs that would otherwise be associated with offering products for sale that are rarely sold.

As an aside, Anderson's book also clears up a popular misunderstanding about the 80-20 rule. Most people incorrectly assume that the 80 and the 20 can be added together. Wrong. The 80 and the 20 come from different denominators; the fact that they are also mathematical complements is sheer coincidence. Thus, it is not wrong to talk about a 90-20 rule or a 70-10 rule if that is what you observe in your own organisation.

---

26 Anderson, C., 2006, *The Long Tail*, Hachette Books.
27 Porter, M. E., 2001, 'Strategy and the Internet', *Harvard Business Review*, Vol. 79, No. 3, pp. 62–78.

4.16 BUYING CENTRE ROLES

This model is one of the simplest, yet profound. Rarely is anything of significant value purchased at the whim of one person. Typically, several people influence a decision to purchase your product, join your club or sign up for your services.

The diagram in **Figure 4.15** says it all. It applies to most business transactions, and frequently domestic purchases too.

Figure 4.15
Buying Centre
Roles.

Much has been written about roles in the buying process,[28] but it pretty much boils down to this. Ask yourself not only who is the buyer but who will use it, where the purchase decision might begin, who (and how) you can influence from elsewhere in the company and who makes the final decision.

Consider a business selling accounting software to small businesses. Whilst the founder of a client company might be an influencer, and likely the buyer too, they are unlikely to be the user; whilst the decider is likely to be the accountant or financial director. For a more domestic example, it's well-known that kids exert an influence on the purchase of the family vehicle.

Often the tricky part is deciding where to start – who will initiate the search, or with whom should we initiate the conversation if we want to sell to the firm? In the particular case of face-to-face selling, the salesperson could do well to consider the culture of the organisation they are approaching first. In a hierarchical organisation, it is frequently very difficult for users to make purchase recommendations, in which case a "top-down" approach is more likely to be successful.

---

28 Kotler, P., 1969, *Marketing Management*, Prentice Hall, Upper Saddle River.

4.17 BUYER READINESS AND THE PURCHASE FUNNEL

Marketing is frequently framed as a matching of customer needs with business offerings. But this static conception overlooks the fact that customers generally go through a *process* before choosing to purchase a product.

The Hierarchy of Effects, also known as the *Purchase Funnel*, is an attempt to conceptualise what's going on during this process – for each individual customer. The adoption curve which we will meet next applies this to an entire market.

Several examples are shown in **Figure 4.16**: Alternative Purchase Models.

The Hierarchy of Effects is a conceptual model outlining customers' progress from becoming aware of a brand or product to deciding to purchase it. There are several versions, but perhaps, the earliest, known by its acronym *AIDA*, was developed by Elmo Lewis in 1898 and was focused on personal selling. AIDA stands for Attention-Interest-Desire-Action.

Figure 4.16
Alternative
Purchase Models.

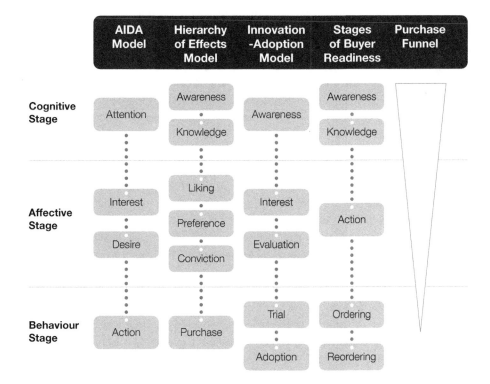

Every few years somebody publishes an article laced with controversial clickbait saying that the Funnel is Dead or the Marketing Hierarchy of Effects is no longer a hierarchy. Many writers may make very good observations or draw sound conclusions, but they frequently miss the point. As with all of the models in this book, they are models. And this means that they are designed to help us make sense of the world. *Management models aren't predictions; they aren't exact analogues of "real life"; and they never claimed to be accurate 100% of the time.* With the funnel, the "issues" are obvious – people don't move in one direction; sometimes they move so fast from awareness to purchase that they barely seem to pause at the milestones along the way. Based on this insight, many businesses – especially those selling online – have invested successfully in techniques to push us through the funnel: from "people are looking at this" and "selling fast" to targeted offers and promotions.

For Internet-based selling, the Purchase Funnel is also used very specifically to describe the process of how the customer works through an online store or sign-up process. In a data-rich environment this gives rise to *funnel metrics* – something which is quite difficult to emulate in an offline world.

4.18 THE ADOPTION CURVE

The adoption curve (also known as the new technology adoption curve or the diffusion of innovation curve) bears an unfortunate visual resemblance to the product lifecycle. But – beware – the two are very different.

Whilst the product lifecycle is a theoretical rule of thumb, the existence of an adoption curve is a matter of fact for every product – even if its exact shape is hard to establish. The adoption curve shows the volume of customers signing up to a new product over time until all the customers who will ever sign up have done so.

The concept of the adoption curve was first proposed by Everett Rogers in 1962.[29] He suggested that for a typical product, distinct segments would emerge which could be characterised by different psychological characteristics and attitudes towards the product. He also suggested the percentage distributions shown in our diagram.

The mistake managers often make is to grossly miscalculate the size and shape of the curve. In the early days of a new product, it is tempting to assume that current buyers are the very tip of a giant adoption curve and that, given time, sales of the product will "automatically" continue to grow and expand to fill its "full" potential. Unfortunately, this just isn't true. A particular challenge of the adoption curve is that it is impossible to identify your place on the curve – at least until adoption growth peaks and begins to slow.

As Geoffrey Moore's *Crossing the Chasm* reminds us,[30] customers at the early stages of the adoption curve think and act very differently to those who come later. In fact, the attitudinal difference is frequently so great that there is little or no natural progression from early adopters to the early majority. (The "chasm" in the title of his book lies between these two groups.)

Building on the findings of Rogers 50 years previously, Moore tells us that those customers who occupy the early stages of the adoption curve are willing to put up with inconvenience or awkwardness.

This is because of their love of the new, their interest in the subject matter, or their allegiance to particular brands and beliefs. The "chasm-crossing" concept has become a popular concept in recent years, to the point where – ironically like

---

29 Rogers, E., 1962, *Diffusion of Innovations*, Free Press, New York.
30 Moore, G., 1991, *Crossing the Chasm: Marketing and Selling Technology Products to Mainstream Customers*, HarperCollins, New York.

the original adoption curve before it – it has created false hope. In a reminder to those establishing new products, Steve Blank has felt compelled to observe:

"The problems you face occur much earlier than any chasm. In fact, you should be so lucky to be dealing with chasm-crossing activities, for they are a sign of success".[31]

Figure 4.17
The Adoption Curve with the Chasm, Incorporating Ideas from Moore (1991).

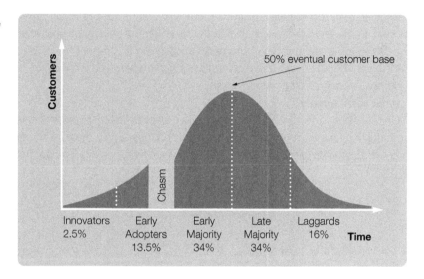

4.19 SUPPLY AND DEMAND

In our web-enabled world, it seems plain ridiculous to suggest that price would ever be regarded as an outcome of the cost of production. But that is what people thought for many years – until Alfred Marshall suggested that price was a function of the interplay between the twin concepts: *supply and demand.*

We'll get back to pricing in **Model 4.12 Pocket Pricing Model**.

Marshall's concepts eventually evolved into the demand curve and supply curve as we typically see them – similar to Figure 4.18. Standard economic theory tells us that the amount of a particular product that is sold *and the price at which it is sold* is a function of both the quantity sought by customers and the quantity available to sell.

In fact, there's equilibrium on the chart where supply and demand intersect. This is the point at which it is neither in the consumers' interest to buy nor in the suppliers' interest to sell any additional units. More on equilibria in **Model 6.4 The Prisoners' Dilemma**.

A couple of points that trip up the novice or you may have forgotten from your studies:

1. Although referred to as a curve, it is usually drawn as a straight line. More on this in a moment.

---

31 Blank, S., 2007, *Four Steps to the Epiphany*, Café Press.

2. Quantity is on the x-axis. In fact, supply and demand are pretty much the only charts where quantity is commonly shown on the x-axis. The reasons for it have been lost in the annals of time.

Let's start with **demand**.

If we look at the model in more detail, we can see that volume demanded increases as price decreases – or put another way, higher prices mean fewer units sold. Consumers will switch to substitutes when the price goes up. We all know this as a general principle from experience: *even if you really wanted to eat at a particular restaurant, there is probably a point where you would deem it too expensive and go elsewhere.*

What about **supply**?

On the supply side, the direction of the curve slopes the other way. At times of oversupply, prices will drop, and when demand outstrips supply, there's a strong incentive for suppliers to stop whatever else they were doing and start producing.

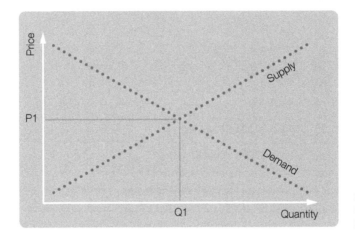

Figure 4.18
Supply and Demand.

The shape of the curve tells us there are only two ways of increasing the quantity sold. One is to reduce the price (moving along the curve), whilst the other is to increase demand at a particular price (shifting the slope out to the right). Demand can be increased through marcoms and advertising (sometimes referred to as "demand generation") and through the presence of complementary products (known as complements). When everyone has a phone with Bluetooth, it's hardly surprising that the demand for Bluetooth headphones goes up.

The inverse of complements are substitutes that drive down demand. In the early days of the Covid-19 pandemic, video conferencing software was viewed as an effective substitute for air travel. We'll meet complements and substitutes again within **Model 6.3 The Value Net**.

One consequence of the supply and demand model is that it sets up the idea that the quantity bought and the price paid are negatively correlated. And this gives rise to the intuition that if more of a product is available, then buyers will expect to pay less for it. This often isn't strictly true but is a good rule of thumb.

It's worth remembering that the demand curve is a theoretical concept that is rarely observable. Even if you can source the data, you'll find that the linear conception of the typical demand curve graph is a dramatic over-simplification, since *consumers tend to be more price-sensitive at the cheaper end, and less so at the more expensive end.* (In other words, the demand line should become shallower as the price drops, towards the right of the diagram.)

In fact, price increases within the Consumer Price Index (CPI; the standard measure of inflation) will often be tolerated, but beyond this they are frequently rejected. Many consumers experience sticker shock at some arbitrary point where something just seems too expensive. And then there are products for which demand actually increases as the price increases – the elusive "Veblen goods" (status symbols where the price is part of the brand) and "Giffen goods" (cheaper items with few substitutes).

4.20 DEMAND ELASTICITY

When you hear people using the terms "Demand Elasticity" or "Price Elasticity", they are typically referring to what economists call "Price Elasticity of Demand". The point is that it is actually the demand that has the characteristic of being elastic, not the price which is the independent variable. It's more commonly termed "price sensitivity".

Price Elasticity of Demand is the effect that an incremental delta (or "change") in price has on the quantity demanded. In other words, it's the angle of the demand curve in the supply and demand model which we met on the previous page.

The price elasticity of demand formula is:

Elasticity = percentage change in quantity / percentage change in price

Products are said to be price inelastic if quantities bought don't change much when the price goes up (a steep curve), and price elastic if even a small change in price causes quantities to change (a flatter curve).

Reduced price elasticity is one of the characteristics of a strong brand, as noted in **Model 4.21 Market-Based Assets**.

We saw in **Model 4.19 Supply and Demand** how moving along the curve with lower prices should result in more sales. Markets typically experience a reduction in cost base over time (see **Model 5.2 The Experience Curve**), so if the product remains relevant and the lower cost is passed on to buyers in the form of lower prices, then more units will sell.

Note how incremental innovation is often passed on to consumers in the form of declining prices. The demand curve predicts that as prices drop, consumers will automatically purchase more. Witness how, as cars have got cheaper, we have more of them – on the roads, in garages, and in car parks. In this way, incremental innovation drives GDP, but not unit profitability.

So how are you going to use this model? Our bet is that you're not. Beware: this is just a theory. Elasticity, like the whole supply and demand model, is often difficult to work within practice.

In a perfect world, price elasticity should be based on how a given group of customers respond to a percentage change in price. But in reality, it's almost impossible to observe the same individuals or clients buying varying volumes of a product at different price points (and even if you could, it's not clear what you would do with this information). Instead, you may be able to draw up a rough curve by throwing different prices at groups of customers, or from researching a sample. But the best it's going to give you is a historical calculation that's assumed to apply in the future. It's also difficult to accurately model the impact on demand of competition or alternative products (this is known as cross-price elasticity; back to substitutes again; **Figure 4.19**).

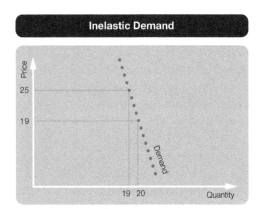
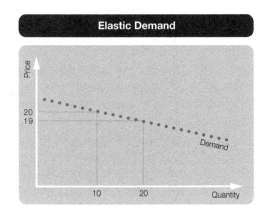

We saw earlier that one of the flaws in the Demand curve is that it is commonly shown linearly but rarely is as straightforward. This means that elasticity will probably be different at different points along the line. Point elasticity is a term sometimes used to capture elasticity for a particular price; that is, the percentage change in demand for a percentage change in price from base price £x or €y.

If you want to predict sales volumes from price, a more practical framework might be **Model 4.13 Pricing Sensitivity Meter**.

Another type of demand elasticity is Income Elasticity of Demand. This refers to the truism that how wealthy you are impacts what and how much you will buy. If you travel between countries that have very different annual salaries, you will have experienced this first-hand, as you compare a road full of SUVs in New York with a street of bicycles and tuk-tuks in Bangkok.

Figure 4.19
Highly Price
Inelastic Demand
and Highly Price
Elastic Demand.

4.21 MARKET-BASED ASSETS

In many businesses, this concept is poorly articulated. Most of us have heard of the concept of "intangible assets" but that's often as far as it goes. And in any case intangible assets were often unattractive because they never appeared on a balance sheet, except to justify why you'd just paid over the odds for an acquisition.

Much as we found the concept of "brand" useful, it clearly wasn't the whole picture either.

When we came across R. K. Srivastava's[32] work in this area the fog cleared. Finally, here was a comprehensive way to think about the company value that existed amongst – and because of – your customers.

Srivastava et al. tell us that the role of marketing is to build market-based assets which in turn will deliver value to the organisation. Like all assets, they should be "cultivated and leveraged". Market-based assets are by definition intangible, but they are without a doubt significant factors in the ongoing success of many leading companies. **Figure 4.20**: Market-Based Assets shows what they are.

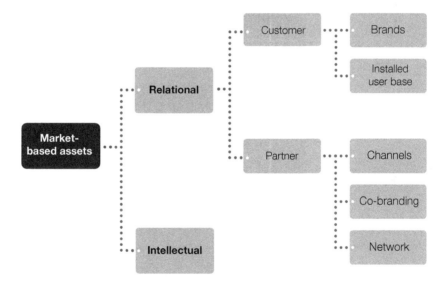

Figure 4.20
Market-Based
Assets. This Figure
Builds upon the
Ideas Expressed
in Srivastava et al.
(1998).

A frequent misconception is to think all market-based assets reside in the minds of customers. Watch out for this sleight of hand by brand valuation firms who like to attribute all intangible asset value to brand equity. But in many cases, relationships (with customers and complementors) and knowledge (in the form of market intelligence gathered by the organisation) can be even more valuable.

---

32 Srivastava, R. K. et al., January 1998, 'Market-Based Assets and Shareholder Value: A Framework
    for Analysis', *Journal of Marketing*, Vol. 62, No. 1, pp. 2–18.

Srivastava's more subtle conception is that market-based assets result from "the co-mingling of the organisation and the environment".

The seminal 1998 paper which introduced the concept lists several ways in which organisations can capture value from market-based assets. Many of these boil down to increased confidence about future cash flows, see **Figure 4.21**: Three Levels of Market-Based Value. They are also likely to deliver the elusive "moats" that we sought in **Model 3.4 Sources of Competitive Advantage**. Just as other types of assets can deliver dividends, so can market-based ones.

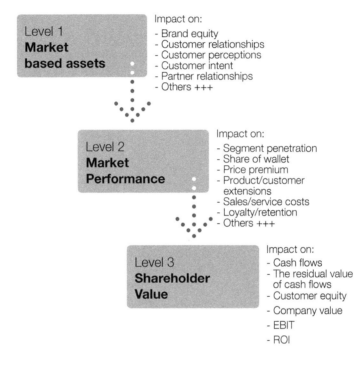

Figure 4.21
Three Levels of Market-Based Value. Republished with permission of Sage Publications Inc., from Srivastava et al. (1998); permission conveyed through Copyright Clearance Center, Inc.

The role of marketing activity is to create market-based assets. Note that "marketing" is not defined as limited to what's done in the marketing department.

4.22 CUSTOMER-CENTRIC REASONS FOR FAILURE

To cap off our section on customers, we thought that a helpful summary from Madhavan Ramanujam and Georg Tacke's *Monetizing Innovation*[33] might be useful. This is a book we met earlier in **Model 4.14 Pricing Sensitivity Meter Redux**.

In their excellent book on monetising new products, the authors claim that there are only four reasons why innovations fail – and it turns out that in some

---

33 Ramanujam, M., & Tacke, G., 2016, *Monetizing Innovation*, Wiley, Hoboken.

way, all relate to customers. Either because the organisation has failed to invest in engaging with and communicating to its client base, or because the product just doesn't fit with what the customer wants. In the worst case, a product tries to solve a problem that no one actually has!

This echoes Steve Blank's observation about causes of failure generally being external to the organisation.

Feature Shock	Cramming too many features into one product - sometimes even unwanted features - creates a product that does not fully resonate with customers and is often overpriced
Minivation	An innovation that, despite being the right product for the right market, is priced too low to achieve its full revenue potential
Hidden Gem	A potential blockbuster product that is never properly brought to market, generally because it falls outside of the core business
Undead	An innovation that customers don't want but has nevertheless been brought to market, either because it was the wrong answer to the right question, or an answer to a question no one was asking

Figure 4.22
Why Products Fail, from Ramanujam and Tacke (2016) Copyright © 2016 by Simon-Kucher & Partners Strategy and Marketing Consultants, LLC. All rights reserved. Reprinted with permission of John Wiley & Sons, Inc.

5   Analysis / Context

No organisation exists in a vacuum. As well as the "jungle" of others competing for customers or suppliers and choosing to cooperate for mutual advantage, there are other factors at play, both upstream and downstream of the company.

In this section we also consider the *stage* or the *maturity* of the organisation within its environment.

If the time is not right, the invention will not take off. Just see how tech resistance or non-availability of materials or adjacent technology holds it back. History is littered with ideas that were conceptually on track but unable to be built or commercialised – from Da Vinci's helicopter to electric cars of the 19th Century that ultimately succumbed to the internal combustion engine.

Similarly, government policy can radically change the environment. Prior to the industrial revolution, the British government issued laws banning finishing machines for woollen fabric, knitting frames, ribbon looms, and the 1562 Statute of Artificers was introduced to regulate who could practice a trade. But by the 19th century, the mood had turned: restrictions were out and the government was now on the side of technology and entrepreneurs – a mood which has largely persisted across Europe and wider afield till the present day.[1]

We'll return to some of these ideas when we talk about product-market fit in **Model 4.5 The Job-to-Be-Done and Outcome-Driven Innovation**.

WHAT TO LOOK OUT FOR

The first big mistake when it comes to context is to ignore it altogether. If your management team is ploughing on, blinkers on, without regard to the world around it, then clearly something is wrong. If the PESTLE analysis just sits, forgotten, on a PowerPoint slide, then why did you do it?

Another challenge comes from using the wrong analogy for your business or misunderstanding the stage you are at. Timing is a big factor in success.

---

1 Mokyr, J., 1990, *The Lever of Riches*, Oxford University Press, New York, pp. 256–258.

DOI: 10.4324/9781003038276-5

And you generally can't control it. But you can be aware of it. Are you ahead of the curve, or behind it? Are you in a new market, or an existing one? Once you've got that sorted, you can form some reasonable hypotheses (customers will or won't easily accept our product; the economy will or won't improve) and use this as the basis for planning how to act and what to look at next.

5.1 PESTLE

PESTLE, rather like **Model 2.1 SWOT**, used to be a feature in every syndicate project at business school. Like SWOT it's a useful little mnemonic, but fortunately it isn't quite as dangerous in the wrong hands as SWOT; so, anyone can use it easily and safely to structure their ideas. In fact, we would say that PESTLE is probably the ultimate tool for thinking about context.

To use PESTLE, draw up a table similar to **Figure 5.1** and fill it out as best you can – ideally based on facts (which can be backed up) rather than opinions. Like SWOT, it helps if you are clear about the context for the analysis – often this might just be "our company over the next five years" but if there are more specific issues on the table ("our continued growth outside of the United States"), it helps to make that explicit.

Figure 5.1
PESTLE Analysis.

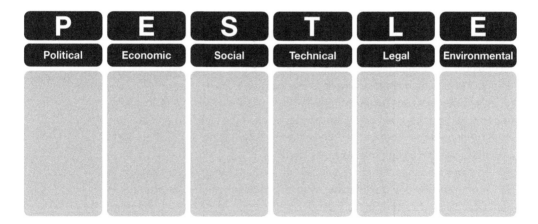

5.2 THE EXPERIENCE CURVE

The concept of an experience curve is loosely based on the notion of a learning curve which preceded it by over a hundred years. Both make the point that things tend to get quicker and easier the more times they are carried out.

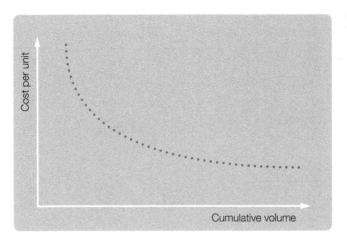

Figure 5.2
The Experience
Curve.

Mokyr writes that "in 1900, an incandescent bulb cost one fifth of what it had 20 years earlier and was twice as efficient".[2] We can see this type of declining price in everything from cars to space rockets to photovoltaic solar panels – it's not just because of an enormous volume discount from the manufacturers; they actually *do* get cheaper to make.

The entry of the experience curve into the business lexicon is generally attributed to Bruce Henderson, the founder of Boston Consulting Group. In the 1960s, Henderson's team researched the concept and concluded that as tasks were duplicated or scaled up, the cost of performing the tasks fell dramatically. The team also claimed the experience curve showed why firms with a large market share tended to be more profitable.

There are several reasons why experience produces efficiency gains. These are learning, discontinuous technological improvement (significant step ups in technology) and economies of scale. The last of these can deliver particularly dramatic results for manufacturing organisations.

Many organisations factor learning-by-doing into their pricing and cost models. For example, it's been documented that firms in the aircraft-manufacturing industry price below cost at first, because they are hoping to get their costs down by achieving a large market share later.[3]

The idea of assuming costs will fall will be familiar to those involved in early-stage technology businesses, where a relatively high-cost strategy is deployed early while the delivery model hasn't been resolved. The so-called "concierge product" is very expensive to run, but is priced on the assumption that the cost to support it will be reduced as human capital is replaced with technology.

---

2 Mokyr, J., 1990, *The Lever of Riches*, p. 126.

3 Benkard, L., 2000, 'Learning and Forgetting: The Dynamics of Aircraft Production', *American Economic Review*, Vol. 90, No. 4, pp. 1034–1054.

5.3 PRODUCT LIFECYCLE

The familiar hump-shaped product lifecycle looks deterministic – suggesting that everything which is born grows steadily and, after a peak, fades out. While there is undoubtedly much truth in this as a rule of thumb, it encourages managers to make assumptions about how growth might occur, and about the inevitability of demise. The product lifecycle is also isolationist: it captures nothing about the relationship between the product and the market within which it sits. Nevertheless, it is useful which is why we include it here.

A fundamental principle that the product lifecycle borrows from the natural world is the notion of competitive exclusion. Russian naturalist Georgii Gause observed that different entities with the same attributes cannot survive alongside each other in the same environment forever.[4] His "law" is sometimes paraphrased as "complete competitors cannot coexist" and explains why differentiation and niche entry is so important. Adaptive species will thrive, like a strain of flu that has mutated so that a vaccine cannot hold it back.

One consequence of this "law" is the way that the players in a market operate with regard to one another as a market matures. Early on, many businesses look similar (often "me toos" are created purely as an attempt to grab a share of the growing pie as markets expand). In more mature markets – in line with Gause's law – few competitors look identical. And, when they start to look similar, they often acquire each other.

Of course, there is room for new operators – but these frequently take a different approach. Drawing on models covered elsewhere in this book, examples include:

- Disruptive innovators – see **Model 7.5 Disruptive Innovation**
- Niche players that have a deep relationship with a small part of the market. We saw what a Niche brand looks like in **Model 4.8 BAV**
- Niche players that have approached the market differently – see **Model 5.4 Blank's Market Types**

Is it a certainty that every product will die? This question is not easy to answer in absolute terms, since the modern conception of a mass-produced, standardised product has only been around for a couple of hundred years. But what *is* clear is that without renewal, most products fade over time, and many of them snuff out completely, particularly if they don't keep abreast of market trends or technological change. Innovation – or a portfolio approach, where a fading star is relaunched or replaced by something new (as we saw in **Model 1.4 The Growth-Share Matrix**) – is a wise insurance policy.

A variant on the product lifecycle in microcosm is the software development lifecycle (sometimes shortened to SDLC). In a nutshell, continuous innovation or continuous improvement is required to ensure that software stays up to date

---

[4] Gause, G. F., 1934, *The Struggle for Existence*, The Williams & Wilkins Company, Baltimore.

and relevant. As one release or version is launched, the next is already being prepared to replace it.

Our table – which is based on a summary by Maximilian Claessens[5] – although you can find many similar tables in lots of marketing textbooks – shows likely tactics and characteristics at different points in the product lifecycle.

Like all models, it is a guide only. It should be *referred to with caution* and is not recommended as a guarantee of what will or should play out at each stage. In this case, rule-based thinking (dangerous in the wrong hands where marketing

Figure 5.3
Product Lifecycle.
Adapted with
permission from
Claessens, M.,
www.marketing-
insider.eu.

Managing Products at Different Stages of the Product Lifecycle

		Introduction	Growth	Maturity	Decline
Characteristics	Sales	Low	Rapidly Increasing	Large but slowing	Declining
	Profits	Negative	Increasing	Large but slowing and subject to attack	Declining or negative
	Customers	Innovators	Early Adopters	Mass-market (Early & Late Majority)	Laggards
	Competition	Few Competitors	Increasing as segment is identified as attractive	Intense — mass marketers	Some are exiting or acquiring
Strategies and Tactics	Marketing Strategy	Market Development	Market Penetration	Defensive Positioning	Efficency or exit
	The Product	Basic and undifferentiated	Developing — product improvement & extension	Differentiated	Fully developed — rationalising range
	Pricing Strategy	Niche: high price; Volume: penetration; Maybe cost-plus	Lowering over time; price for penetration	Lowest; competitor pricing	Increasing
	Promotion	Product awarness	Brand awareness	Brand loyalty	Reinforcement
	Sales Promotion	Heavy sales activity to drive trial (eg freemium, referral)	Reduce selling — exploit increasing demand	Increased selling — to encourage brand switching	Reduce selling costs to retain profitability in sunset

5 Claessens, M., 2015, Product Lifecycle Strategies (PLC) and Characteristics – Managing Each PLC Stage, *Marketing Insider*, https://marketing-insider.eu/product-life-cycle-strategies/

is concerned) could lead you to kill off a product prematurely or cause the early destruction of value by failure to support a promising product. In 1976, Dhalla and Yuspeh published a now long-forgotten paper[6] in *Harvard Business Review* pointing out that product lifecycle was full of "myths of class and form" and that it "leads managers to kill off brands that could be profitable for many more years". The "decline" phase of the product lifecycle can be self-fulfilling: reduce spending and watch the product die.

Cycles apply to countries and larger economies too. Cardwell's law[7] suggests that countries rise and fall just like products do. Donald Cardwell wrote, "no nation has been very creative for more than an historically short period. Fortunately, as each leader has flagged there has always been, up to now, a nation or nations that take over the torch". If true this means that the USA is destined to fall behind other countries at some point – or at least require superhuman effort to break out of the cycle by holding on to its technical pre-eminence.

5.4 BLANK'S MARKET TYPES

A lot of nonsense is talked about new products. Much of it stems from managers treating new products like ones that are already successful (No, Amazon's marketplace of 150M users is not a good analogy for your unlaunched, radical idea). Still more comes from failing to consider the vastly different environments which different products seek to enter. (MySpace, Facebook and TikTok might occupy a similar sector, but they were launched in very different circumstances.)

There are no rules of thumb when it comes to new products. At the turn of the century, the iPod was introduced with PR and a tightly controlled channel to market. Over a decade later the iPad was launched – on the back of the iPhone – quickly in mass media and mainstream retail. Meanwhile Android overtook the iPhone years ago with almost no promotion of its own but some channel partners that stood to gain enormously from its success (namely Samsung). The dynamics of the market and the behaviour of competitors in it govern what will work.

Getting the approach wrong can lead to costly mistakes and lost ground to rivals. Steve Blank is a Stanford academic and an entrepreneur of some repute. He suggests that managers consider three market types for a new product:[8]

- An existing market
- A new market where there are no competitors
- A re-segmented (existing) market, where the new product is positioned as

6 Dhalla, N. K., & Yuspeh, S., 1976, 'Forget the Product Life Cycle Concept!', *Harvard Business Review*, Vol. 54, pp. 102–112.

7 Cardwell, G., 1972, *Turning Points in Western Technology; A Study of Technology, Science and History*, Science History Publishing, New York.

8 Blank, S., 2005, *Four Steps to the Epiphany*. He subsequently added a fourth type, 'the Clone market'.

a niche player or a low-price alternative

Blank's "types" are about both external circumstances the firm faces and how the company chooses to see itself.

For an existing market, the primary commercial objective is to take a share from incumbents. In a new market, the share is irrelevant. Blank says, "Therefore spending money on a massive launch to generate customers and market share is ludicrous". New markets are generally better served by quieter, focused growth activities.

In a re-segmentation situation, the commercial task is both about the share and about re-education; encouraging customers to see themselves and their market in a new way. Foursquare, which ran the risk of being lumped in with giants like Facebook, deliberately created a new subcategory of location-based services, although its time had passed while Facebook went on to embrace much of the same functionality.

It's worth remembering the old marketing adage reflected in Ries and Ries's *Law of the Category*: "If you can't be first in a category, set up a new category you can be first in".[9]

Figure 5.4
Blank's Market Types. Adapted with permission from Blank, S., *Four Steps to the Epiphany*.

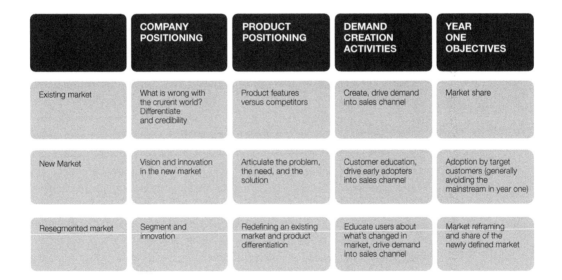

	COMPANY POSITIONING	PRODUCT POSITIONING	DEMAND CREATION ACTIVITIES	YEAR ONE OBJECTIVES
Existing market	What is wrong with the crurent world? Differentiate and credibility	Product features versus competitors	Create, drive demand into sales channel	Market share
New Market	Vision and innovation in the new market	Articulate the problem, the need, and the solution	Customer education, drive early adopters into sales channel	Adoption by target customers (generally avoiding the mainstream in year one)
Resegmented market	Segment and innovation	Redefining an existing market and product differentiation	Educate users about what's changed in market, drive demand into sales channel	Market reframing and share of the newly defined market

Blank reminds us that when early-stage products fail, they tend to go wrong because they don't have a market willing to buy the product at the right price, at the right time and in sufficient numbers. We saw in **Model 4.22 Customer-Centric Reasons for Failure** that product performance or dodgy technology is rarely the reason. We'll return to this in our summary of Blank's other key framework in **Model 7.9 Customer Development**.

---

9 Ries, A., & Ries, L., 1998, *The 22 Immutable Laws of Branding*.

6 Analysis / Competitors and Complementors

For the last part of the Analysis section, we've lumped together Competitors and Complementors. This is deliberate, since a company may play the twin roles of competitor and complementor at the same time.

Whether perfect substitutes or imperfect ones, most organisations face some form of competition. And as we have seen, competition tends to become fiercer as markets mature and there is less "food" to go around.

Many organisations also find that their value is enhanced by other businesses. Variously known as contextual activation, network effects and ecosystem effects, the concept here is that an independent entity can create value for your business *without* a direct commercial relationship.

Belkin and Logitech have a long history of promoting Apple's various portable devices through peripherals – starting with docks for the iPod, followed by assorted enhancements to iPhone and latterly keyboards and cases for the iPad.

For examples of companies that enhance each other's value whilst competing ferociously at the same time, we need to look no further than today's technology titans: Apple computers continue to benefit from Microsoft software such as Word and Excel, and Microsoft happily creates apps that run on Apple's Mac OS at the same time as its own Windows suite offers an end-to-end alternative. Google's Android division provides an alternative to Apple iOS at the same time as the two companies cooperate on Covid-tracing apps, interoperability of virtual assistants; and Apple benefits from the availability of Google maps on the iPhone. The little-known but highly influential Zigbee Alliance is working on standards for the connected home. Its board includes representatives from all three of the major smart speaker brands, plus many components and device manufacturers.[1]

---

1 https://zigbeealliance.org/members/

DOI: 10.4324/9781003038276-6

WHAT TO LOOK OUT FOR

It may sound obvious, but the biggest mistake you can make here is to ignore other companies in the market or fail to understand who the true substitutes, competitors (and complementors) are. Think critically on this point – could that company be persuaded to complement us? Could that partner eventually "go direct" and compete, perhaps buoyed by the learnings they've had at our side?

Losses loom large, and a business under threat may prove a formidable opponent in battle. Do you really want to poke the bear?

Success is not a state of mind. *You actually have to be better than your competitors*. Keeping up with peers operationally isn't enough. When Porter spoke about the "productivity frontier", he was making the point that – for any given point of technical evolution – there is a theoretical maximum productivity at every price. You can't keep pushing that out. If you don't have a competitive advantage, don't compete. You will only end up closer and closer to the edge of what's possible, which just means a suicidal battle of price and margins.

6.1 SO YOU THINK YOU'RE A CHALLENGER?

We know from **Model 5.3 Product Lifecycle** that the best way to enter a mature market is by picking off a niche segment or providing a product that is very different to what's currently offered. This is frequently described as being a "challenger" brand or business.

Adam Morgan published *Eating the Big Fish* in 2009, a bible for firms that see themselves as challengers.[2] He urges companies not to hide behind the term but to be really specific about what it means to them.

As markets mature, it's perhaps not surprising that firms who don't lead their particular markets start describing themselves as "challengers". When you hear a firm referring to itself as a "challenger" (or if you are tempted to describe your own organisation in this manner), ask yourself the following questions:

- What are we challenging?
- How are we challenging?

For a firm that has been around for a while, be super-critical. Is "challenger" simply an excuse for poor performance, inadequate promotional budgets or

---

2 Morgan, A., 2009, *Eating the Big Fish: How Challenger Brands Can Compete against Brand Leaders*, Wiley.

a losing battle being fought against a better-connected competitor? There is clear market space for a genuine challenger in many markets and Morgan's list shows how it can be done. But for the pretender, the writing may already be on the wall.

CHALLENGER STANCE	EXAMPLE	DESCRIPTION	CHALLENGING WHAT?
People's Champion	Virgin Mobile	On your side, against the fat cats	Motives of the leader
Feisty Underdog	Under Armour	Sticking it to Goliath	The big, the evil, the 'them'
Irreverent Maverick	Brewdog	Counter-cultural attitude in a box	Narrow-mindedness of the category
Dramatic Disrupter	Sniffe & Likkit	An offer significantly superior to the incumbent	How we've always done it
Enlightened Zagger	Bundy	Deliberately swimming against the cultural tide	The assumptions of the category
Missionary	Dove	Looking to put things right – a view to share	The beliefs of the category
Real & Human	Mailchimp	A 'real' player in an impersonal category	The facelessness of the leader
Local Hero	Bookshop.org	Understanding local needs	The global and generic offerings
Democratiser	IKEA	Making the previously exclusive more widely avaiable	Elitism and restricted access
Next Generation	NotCo, Beyond Meat	Perfect for the times we live in today	Outdated assumptions of the category

Figure 6.1
Challenger Brands. Adapted from the Work of Adam Morgan, eatbigfish and PHD with permission. For further information see www.eatbigfish.com.

6.2 THE HALF-TRUTH OF FIRST MOVER ADVANTAGE

It's tempting to think the concepts "first mover" and "advantage" go together naturally. In fact, being the first mover is not always as good as it's cracked up to be. In fact, according to Suarez and Lanzolla,[3] when technology is evolving rapidly, the players that emerge once the pace of change begins to slow are often those who succeed.

For firms considering new innovations it is particularly important to consider where their market and underpinning technology are on this framework.

The "calm waters" quadrant is the optimal combination of slowly changing technology and slow market movement.

Here, timing is everything. Advantage can come from an element of surprise or the opportunity to become the de-facto standard. Elsewhere, much can be learned from watching other entrants, similar firms or those in adjacent sectors.

Suarez and Lanzolla's Harvard Business Review paper *The Half-Truth of First Mover Advantage* suggests that if technology – or the market – moves quickly, then first mover advantage might be short-lived because of rapid obsolescence or changing customer behaviour. On the other hand, it is when change is slow that first mover advantage actually materialises. The article was written before the platform behemoths of recent years (Amazon, eBay, Shopify, Facebook, etc.), but it is still food for thought.

Take Uber. Definitely a first mover on the global stage. And in terms of share of mind and share of PR, they seem to have won. (Uber recently declared its first quarterly profit in late 2021, 12 years after launch.)

Figure 6.2
First Mover Advantage. Adapted with permission of Harvard Business Publishing from Suarez and Lanzolla, "The Half-Truth of First-Mover Advantage", April 2005, Harvard Business Review. Copyright ©2005 Harvard Business Publishing; all rights reserved.

---

3 Suarez, F., & Lanzolla, G., 2005, 'The Half-Truth of First-Mover Advantage', *Harvard Business Review*, Vol. 83, No. 4, pp. 121–127.

There's another term "first to scale" which is sometimes used in place of first mover. This can be helpful as there are frequently multiple early movers (so it is difficult to see who is really first), and often a technical breakthrough isn't commercialised for some years.

In 1969, Douglas Engelbart demonstrated several concepts that might become features of computers in the future. Subsequently known as the "Mother of All Demos",[4] the presentation featured live demonstrations of the mouse, the graphical user interface, video conferencing, hyperlinks and screen sharing. None of these products had commercial success for at least a decade. Similarly, Xerox is the name often cited as the pioneer of the modern graphical user interface, but you wouldn't really regard them as first in any meaningful market-facing sense.

6.3 THE VALUE NET

Competitors, Collaborators, Complementors?

Brandenberger and Nalebuff weren't the only people to notice that in the past 15 years the way companies behave towards each other has started to change, but they were the first to link it to a new buzzword: *co-opetition*.[5]

Co-opetition refers to the mix of competitive and cooperative strategies that firms can deploy with each other. Sir Martin Sorrell famously called it "kiss and punch", whilst others use the term "frenemy".

The arrival of the Internet has accelerated the forces of co-opetition in many markets, as it brings former rivals together, changes the economics of existing markets and creates new market opportunities.

So when should two companies compete, and when is it better to cooperate?

Brandenberger and Nalebuff's *Value Net* (Figure 6.3) helps provide some of the answers. Although it's often compared to Porter's Five Forces, the Value Net is a very different way of looking at the world.

The parties in the Value Net are players in a game, the purpose of which is to generate the maximum value for all the players combined. Unlike the Five Forces, parties can occupy several boxes at the same time – that happens when a valuable customer base means customers act as complementors.

Rather than being based on revenue or profitability, the currency of the Value Net is something Brandenberger and Nalebuff call "Added Value". In this context, the phrase has a quite distinct meaning – different from how it is often used to describe some sizzle to go with your sausage. Added Value is not the same as straight-up value (and it's also different to Economic Value-Added which refers to a financial metric[6]).

---

4 It's easy to find this demo on YouTube and well worth watching.

5 Brandenburger, A. M., & Nalebuff, B. J., 1996, *Co-opetition*, Double Day, New York.

6 We've steered clear of Financial Valuation models in this book, but for those who are interested, Economic Value-Added refers to the value created by a business when subtracting its cost of capital from operating profit. This bears no relationship to the concept of Added Value outlined above. Sometimes, it seems word order matters.

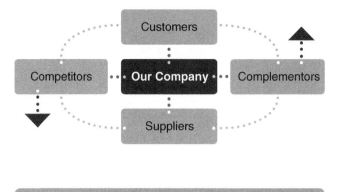

The Added Value of each player in the market (or "game" as Brandenberger and Nalebuff call it) is defined as the difference in the total value of the entire game with that player in the game versus the same game *without* the player involved. It's a good way to think about the value of players that aren't in a straightforward value chain. For example; imagine the market of boutique craft stores without Etsy.com; or manufacturers without Alibaba.com. A player's Added Value also provides us with a rough cap on their bargaining power: the player will not be able to negotiate for a large share of profits than they are bringing in the form of Added Value.

We already met the concepts of substitutes and complements in **Model 4.19 Supply and Demand**. Competitors produce substitutes, and complementors produce complements. In the Value Net, Competitors decrease your Added Value and Complementors have the opposite effect.

Added Value also helps explain why companies seek to cooperate with their peers without charging for the service. It explains why APIs (application protocol interfaces) have become so popular to connect companies – and why they are often made available at no charge or as a feature that is "bundled in" with other services. If my contact management platform can easily connect me to a reporting suite and a bulk email platform, then everyone benefits and everyone makes more money. So, no one charges for the interface itself – at least that's the theory. At the time of writing, several large platform companies do still charge for these types of access because they can; a demonstration of market power in action.

As well as helping firms decide how to treat neighbouring firms, the Value Net also helps companies work out how they want others to behave. Who are your substitutes? And how can you neutralise them? Or better still, turn them into complementors?

Bill Gates is alleged to have said "A platform is when the economic value of everybody that uses it exceeds the value of the company that creates it. Then it's a platform". This means that the platform is more valuable than the company that owns it. This relates to Added Value because if you took a major platform out of a market like selling cars or buying houses (think autotrader.com or carsales. com), everyone would be worse off, for a while at least.

6.4 THE PRISONERS' DILEMMA

Continuing the theme of cooperation, The *Prisoners' Dilemma* was originally presented in 1950 by Merrill Flood and Melvin Dresher to demonstrate how collaboration is often a smarter – if not an entirely obvious or rational – course of action. The complication is that *cooperation only makes sense if the other party also cooperates*.

Intuitively we all know this from the high school playground. Offer to cooperate with a bully and they may bop you on the nose, in which case you will wish you had put up a fight. However, if they cooperate in return, chances are you'll both have an easier time in the schoolyard.

There are lots of versions of the Prisoners' Dilemma, but the basics are as follows: Two prisoners are jointly accused of a crime and are asked, separately, if they would like to confess. It is assumed that the two defendants have acted together, so if one confesses, they are in effect accusing the other of lying. They cannot see what the other has said until after both have answered. If only one confesses, then the confessor is let off and the silent counterpart receives the maximum sentence. If both confess, then they each receive a moderate sentence. And if both are silent, they both receive minimum sentence. In this example, it makes sense for both to accuse the other, since they will either get off (if the other remains silent), or receive two years (if both counter-accuse). Remaining silent is obviously the best outcome, but the risk is simply too great in case the other side speaks out, which rationally they would.

Figure 6.4
The Prisoners' Dilemma (my choices in bold; other's choices in italics).

		Other's choices	
		Silence	*Confess*
My choices	**Silence**	**Minimal sentence (1 year)** *Minimal sentence (1 year)*	**Guilty and lying (3 years)** *Guilty but cooperative (freedom)*
	Confess	**Guilty but cooperative (freedom)** *Guilty and lying (3 years)*	**Guilty but admitting it (2 years)** *Guilty but admitting it (2 years)*

If only both prisoners could guarantee to the other that they will remain silent! A very useful concept when trying to solve the Prisoners' Dilemma is that of **commitment**. Back in the prison, if the prisoners could have agreed not to accuse each other, and found a way to commit to the agreement (perhaps by threatening a visit from angry relatives) then they could stay silent with no risk that they would end up on the receiving end of an accusation.

The mutually silent prisoners get off with minimum sentence by cooperating. But by operating in isolation they will choose to confess, since this is the position that individually trumps all of the others. The double confession is known as the **dominant** or **equilibrium** position, since no one can improve upon it by changing their decision. But it's clearly *not optimal*.

What is the relevance of the Prisoners' Dilemma to a book on management models?

1   It demonstrates why signalling and commitment are important in business. Generally, businesses are forbidden to collude, but they can make public statements or take particular positions that enable adjacent businesses to make assumptions about how they will behave. A CEO of an organisation will frequently go on the record saying that the business "will" or "will not" do something in the future. It might not be a cast-iron guarantee, but it is more likely than not to come to pass. Similarly, a business that shuts down a division or puts it up for sale may be signalling its willingness to cooperate on a joint venture instead.

2   The Prisoners' Dilemma also shows why cooperation can be the logical choice in certain circumstances – if only we set aside our default animosity. This is something that Brandenburger and Nalebuff (remember them from **Model 6.3 The Value Net**?) have written about extensively in their book *Co-opetition*.[7] They give examples of banks refusing to join ATM networks through sheer intransigence; booksellers squabbling over customers when they should have been growing the pie; and on the successful side of the ledger, specialist retailers successfully clustering together in certain districts, and rival computer manufacturers cooperating to fund the development of Java in the early 1990s. If the book were being written today, they would have found many similar examples from the open-source software movement that are funded or supported by rival corporations.

The "prison" metaphor isn't always the easiest to relate to, so **Figure 6.5** has been labelled to demonstrate two parties choosing to trade or go to war. It's not hard to go from this to two organisations choosing to cooperate or go for all-out competition. Thanks go to Steven Pinker[8] on whose work this version is based. Pinker's book *The Better Angels of Our Nature* covers far bigger and more important themes than mere management models – but he does aim to explain why rational humans seek to embrace "gentle commerce" rather than all-out-battle to the finish. In Pinker's model, a profitability dividend has been loaded onto the "Pacifist" Trade/Trade side of the equation so that it has the highest payoff, but an individualist calculus may still choose to go to war to avoid an expensive military defeat.

---

7   Brandenburger, A., & Nalebuff, B., 1996, *Co-opetition*.
8   Pinker, S., 2011, *The Better Angels of Our Nature*, p. 825.

		Other's choices	
		Pacifist	Aggressor
My choices	**Pacifist**	**Peace + Profit (5+100 = 105)** *Peace + Profit (5+100 = 105)*	**Defeat (-100)** *Victory (10)*
	Aggressor	**Victory (10)** *Defeat (-100)*	**War (-50)** *War (-50)*

Figure 6.5
Pinker's "How commerce resolves the Pacifist's Dilemma" (my choices in bold; other's choices in italics) from Figure 10-3 from *The Better Angels of Our Nature: Why Violence Has Declined* by Steven Pinker, copyright © 2011 by Steven Pinker. Used by permission of Viking Books (US) and Allen Lane 2011, Penguin Books 2012 (UK), imprints of Penguin Publishing Group, a Division of Penguin Random House LLC. All rights reserved.

The Prisoners' Dilemma is particularly relevant to price competition. Whilst it may seem attractive to drop prices to take the market share from competitors, if this triggers a price war this may damage the entire industry leaving the instigator with no more market share (and often less). And whilst consumers relish the opportunities to "get a deal" presented by a price war, they don't generally welcome the loss of competition that may eventually result.

It has been suggested that during the US airline price war of 1992, the combined losses that year exceeded the industry's combined profits since inception. American Airlines, Northwest Airlines and other carriers descended into a cycle of retaliatory price cuts.[9] On the other hand, retailers are particularly good at signalling that they don't want price wars – ever wondered by big stores frequently offer to "price match" their competitors? It's a promise to their rivals that *if you go, we go too.*

---

9 Rao, A., Bergen, M., & Davis, S., 2000, 'How to Fight a Price War', *Harvard Business Review*, Vol. 78, No. 2, pp. 107–116.

7   Strategic Planning

Deciding how we'll get there

Strategic decisions are frequently uncomfortable and often ignored – or put off until a tomorrow that never comes.

Decision time is when push comes to shove, when the rubber meets the road, when companies show their mettle.

However, you look at it, decisionmaking is at the very heart of strategy. Decisions have consequences.

Importantly, choosing to follow one path means excluding another. You go this way, a competitor goes another – once the decision is made, some of the things they do will cease to be options for you.

The toughest things in strategy are the things we choose not to do. We usually can't have it both ways, although we often want to.

Go on. Choose.

WHAT TO LOOK OUT FOR

Hope is not a strategy.

A disconnect between vision and the strategic, operational, business or financial plans will render each of them useless. The interlinkages are what makes delivery work. Have you made a choice based on all of the available information? Is it consistently driven down through all levels of the plan? Do people know what to work on? Do they know why? Do they know if it's succeeding?

Stuck in a loop of iteration, the pursuit of theoretical perfection is a vortex from which it may be difficult to escape. Make a choice and then move forward to delivery (which we'll tackle in the next section).

Look out for faux choices: claims like "we've decided to win", "we'll be the most profitable in the industry", or "we've chosen to be customer centric". How? What are the trade-offs? What are we *not* doing?

DOI: 10.4324/9781003038276-7

7.1 PORTER'S GENERIC STRATEGIES

At the most fundamental level, every business has a choice between "buying low" and "selling high". In 1980, Michael Porter introduced the world to the term "generic strategy", along with the four-box diagram based on a simple binary choice between *either* low cost or differentiation, with a broad and focused variant of each. His version has since become one of the most famous strategy models of all time.[1]

The model is simple but frequently misunderstood. Many casual observers talk about generic strategy as a choice between competing on price and being different in some way. In fact, cheap inputs do not automatically lead to low prices, nor should they. And on the other hand, differences that aren't valuable don't count.

There are three important misconceptions:

* Misconception one: "differentiation" means "being different". Remember that Porter is first and foremost an economist and that for him "differentiation" refers to the ability to charge more than for equivalent products.
* Misconception two: "low cost" means "low price" or "charge less". As any accountant will tell you, price and cost don't necessarily go together.
* Misconception three: the options are mutually exclusive – in other words, we do one or the other, but not both. This too, it turns out, is incorrect.

The point of generic strategies is to force a choice. Whilst there are a small number of companies that successfully straddle both low costs and highly valued outputs, they are the exception rather than the rule.

Figure 7.1 is how most people first meet Porter's Generic Strategies. Figure 7.2 helps put the Differentiation and Low Cost options into context. The first point to make here is that differentiation tends to raise the company's costs (think how it costs more to make a fancy motorbike than a basic one) – but not by as much as the premium that the company will be able to charge. This is the essence of any kind of "premium" business strategy – if the cost increment equalled the price increment, then there would be no point.

On the other hand, the low-cost business is *able* to offer a lower price should it wish to. But they might not. In this diagram, we have shown the customer's Willingness to Pay as a *constant* between the lower cost producer and the "typical" producer. Thus, the low-cost operator is able to achieve higher margins. Incidentally, if they can signal their lower cost base to competitors, they may be able to prevent a price war. (See **Model 6.4 The Prisoners' Dilemma** for more on signalling.

---

1 Porter, M. E., 1980, *Competitive Strategy*, Free Press, New York.

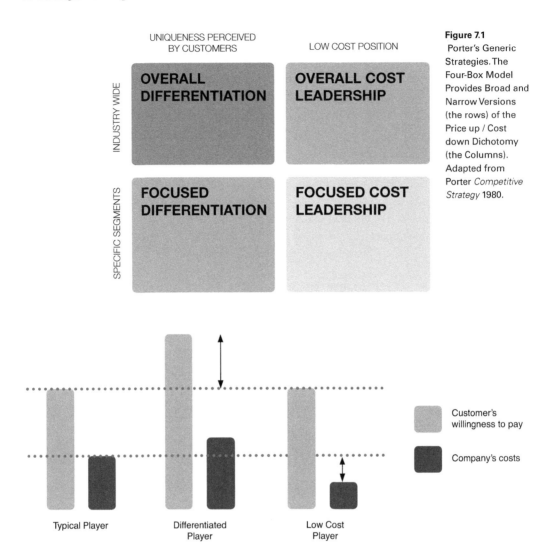

Figure 7.1
Porter's Generic
Strategies. The
Four-Box Model
Provides Broad and
Narrow Versions
(the rows) of the
Price up / Cost
down Dichotomy
(the Columns).
Adapted from
Porter *Competitive
Strategy* 1980.

As Porter famously put it, most companies that try both Low Cost *and* Differentiation will end up "stuck in the middle". There are, however, some examples of businesses that *do* successfully pursue a double strategy; particularly if they can access economies of scale or benefit from the experience curve (see **Model 5.2**) whilst also producing a premium product.

Two examples are Lexus cars (who benefit from the scale advantages of the parent company Toyota) and Apple (who despite a premium positioning continues to manufacture a small number of hardware models or SKUs in extremely large volumes).

Another approach is to segment the product offering and run different strategies in each. A good example is Burger King. You'll never find Burger King's Whopper in a price war because it is (relatively) premium – AKA "differentiated" – whilst the fries market is all about keeping costs down.

Figure 7.2
Differentiation
versus Low-
Cost Strategies.
It Generally
Costs More to
Differentiate, But
If the Increased
Willingness to Pay
Is Ahead of the
Cost Uplift, You Are
Winning.

7.2 THE DISCIPLINE OF MARKET LEADERS

In their 1995 book *The Discipline of Market Leaders*,[2] Treacy and Wiersema say that "no company can succeed today by trying to be all things to all people."

They proposed that all organisations need to choose among three generic approaches (Figure 7.3):

- operational excellence
- product leadership; or
- customer intimacy

Operational excellence is typically about low variability, high volume and low cost. Customer intimacy is hands-on and involves a heavy dose of service, often face-to-face. Product leadership is about products worth paying more for, because they innovate.

In 2000, Kaplan and Norton picked up the theme by identifying the product attributes, relationships and image components of each modus operandi.[3] They also characterised each option in the form of what they call the company's "image". You can think of these as a kind of generic value proposition – a starting point for thinking about why customers buy from any company. For more on this, see **Model 4.3 Value Propositions**.

It's important to note that the characteristics *not* chosen for focus aren't to be ignored altogether. In other words, a company that is geared towards Customer Intimacy can't entirely overlook Product/Service attributes *and so on*. In Kaplan and Norton's diagram, the characteristics that aren't a key focus still get a tick – showing that they can't be discounted entirely.

7.3 BLUE OCEAN STRATEGY

When *Blue Ocean Strategy*[4] first appeared, it seemed to have perfected the art form of seeming both very familiar and brand new at the same time. It made sense as it built on many existing ideas, but it made powerful concepts into simple frameworks. It was an exercise in distillation.

Chan Kim and Renée Mauborgne have published several books and articles that examine strategy through the lens of the "blue ocean".[5] The name is inspired by the concept of escaping the so-called "red ocean" of ferocious rivalry by getting away from similarly positioned competitors. Recall the point made by Gause in **Model 5.3 Product Lifecycle** that "two competitors cannot occupy the same

---

2 Treacy, M., & Wiersema, F., 1997, *The Discipline of Market Leaders: Chose Your Customers, Narrow Your Focus, Dominate Your Market*, Perseus Books.

3 Kaplan, R., & Norton, D., September 2000, 'Having Trouble with Your Strategy? Then Map It', *Harvard Business Review*, Vol. 78, No. 5, pp. 167–176.

4 Kim, C., & Mauborgne, R., 2004, 'Blue Ocean Strategy', *Harvard Business Review*.

5 Kim, C., & Mauborgne, R., 2005, 2015, *Blue Ocean Strategy*, Harvard Business Review Press; 2017, *Blue Ocean Shift*, Hachette, London; www.blueoceanstrategy.com

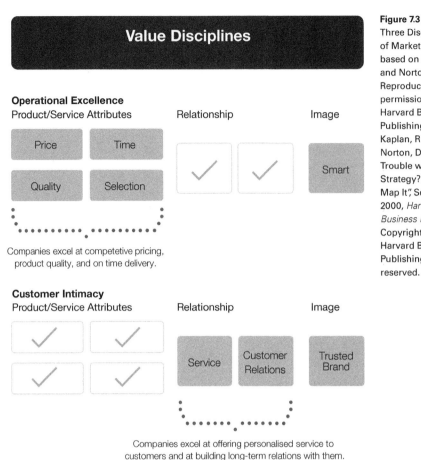

niche indefinitely". Successive generations of companies seem to forget that "red ocean" ends with someone getting eaten.

Figure 7.4 shows two diagrams from *Blue Ocean Strategy*, Chan Kim and Renée Mauborgne's *ERRC Grid* and their *Value Innovation Diamond*. ERRC relates to the four dimensions of value creation – eliminate, reduce, raise or

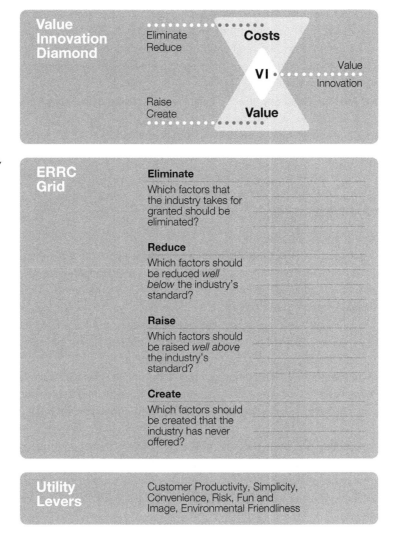

Figure 7.4
Value Innovation
Diamond and
ERRC Grid © Chan
Kim and Renée
Mauborgne,
Republished with
Permission. As
Featured in *Blue
Ocean Strategy*
(Harvard Business
Review Press, 2005,
2015), *Blue Ocean
Shift* (Hachette,
2017), www.
blueoceanstrategy.
com.

create – whilst the value innovation diamond shows that all elements of value creation fall into two categories – cost down or value up.

Sound familiar? Some have said that *Blue Ocean Strategy* is a repackaging of the basic strategic principles of "cost down, value up" which feature in **Model 7.1 Porter's Generic Strategies**. However, as a well-structured aide memoir, it serves a useful purpose.

Eagle-eyed readers may notice that the ERRC elements form the basis of value propositions (see **Models 4.3** and **4.4**) – although within the Value Proposition Canvas, they are simplified to just Gains Created and Pains Relieved. We think that Kim and Mauborgne's ERRC is a better conception. Meanwhile, the notion of reducing performance below the typical level of any industry has echoes of **Model 7.5 Disruptive Innovation**.

Kim and Mauborgne's list of "Utility Levers" is particularly incisive. Customer Productivity, Simplicity, Convenience, Risk (Reduction), Fun and Image, Environmental Friendliness (we might call that "Sustainability") is a checklist which any organisation could do well to consider as they look to win customers from the clutches of competitors.

Kim and Mauborgne's body of work is simply enormous and includes many examples from companies around the world showing how they have pulled away from the pack and successfully moved away from the industry's current focus or current frame of reference.

7.4 BRAND ARCHITECTURE

One face to the market or two?

Brand architecture is the name given to the structure and number of brands through which a business presents itself to the market – to target particular segments or to highlight product differences. Particularly tricky is the nature of the interrelationship between these brands.

Will we publicise the relationship between brands? And if so, to what degree? David Aaker's Brand Relationship Spectrum[6] presents the most commonly used terminology for analysing these relationships.

The fundamental question "when is more than one brand required?" is easy to answer – at least in theory. When a brand is being stretched to breaking point by a diversity of products or product variants, it's time to create something new.

Businesses that operate a portfolio of brands frequently change strategy over time. When Mini was relaunched, it was frequently referred to even in official communications as BMW Mini – a phrase subtly phased out subsequently. Similarly, who hears of *Microsoft* Xbox these days, or *Skoda, part of the Volkswagen group*?

7.5 DISRUPTIVE INNOVATION

"Disruptive innovation" is a phrase that gets bandied about a lot by consultants, journalists and in management meetings. It's generally used sloppily and often refers to a type of challenger brand (see **Model 6.1**), or to the hope that a firm can somehow out-innovate its competitors.

---

6 Aaker, D. A., & Joachminsthaler, E. A., 2000, 'The Brand Relationship Spectrum: The Key to the Brand Architecture Challenge', *California Management Review*, Vol. 42, No. 4, pp. 8–23.

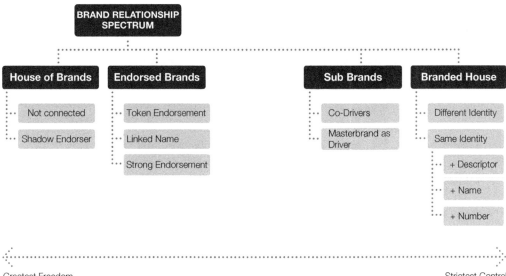

Greatest Freedom   **Strictest Control**

Most Autonomy

Highest Communication Costs

Broadest Range of Product Types

Strictest Control

Highest Integration

Greatest Communications Synergy

Narrower Range of Product Types

Figure 7.5
The Brand
Relationship
Spectrum.
Republished with
permission of
Sage Publications
Inc, from 'The
Brand Relationship
Spectrum: The
Key to the Brand
Architecture
Challenge',
Joachminsthaler,
E., and Aaker,
D. A, *California
Management
Review*, Summer
2000; permission
conveyed through
Copyright Clearance
Center, Inc.

Harvard professor Clayton Christensen certainly doesn't have the monopoly on the term "Disruptive Innovation," but we recommend sticking to his interpretation, which has a very specific meaning.[7] For Christensen, disruptive innovation refers only to ***innovations that offer less functionality than the incumbents they seek to challenge***. (If you're not familiar with Christensen, it's worth reading that sentence twice.)

We met Christensen earlier in **Model 4.5 The Job-to-Be-Done and Outcome-Driven Innovation**. You can see some carry-over between the two key concepts: both are about the problems that organisations solve, and how they solve them.

It's a useful reminder that when considering innovations, it is a mistake to think only in terms of customers who are looking for more. (Incidentally this is yet another reason why it's a mistake to ask customers what they want since almost no one will say they want less.) Many customers who are over serviced may be happy with less functionality, particularly if it can be delivered at a lower price than what they pay currently. The classic path for disruptive innovation is to begin by servicing a small niche market and then to creep up on mainstream alternatives. Sound familiar? This has echoes in **Model 5.3 Product Lifecycle**.

---

7 Bower, J. L., & Christensen, C. M., February 1995, 'Disruptive Technologies Catching the Wave', *Harvard Business Review*, Vol. 73, pp. 43–53.

Time and time again, companies that lead in a particular market have failed to recognise the threat from competitors who approach them in this way, tending to dismiss them as "inferior".

Christensen uses the concept of performance trajectories to explain the role played by disruptive innovations (Figure 7.6). There are two important principles:

- First, the disruptive innovation begins by offering a lower level of performance than the incumbent
- Second, because the performance of both the incumbent and the disruptor is continuously increasing, the performance of the disruptor eventually intersects the level of performance required by the mainstream market

This doesn't work automatically. Early in this century, while smartphone manufacturers were competing to offer more features, Netherlands-based John's Phone launched with no screen, no qwerty keyboard and certainly no internet browser. And guess what? It flopped. But the market for this type of phone aimed at small children catching public transport to school seems more promising.

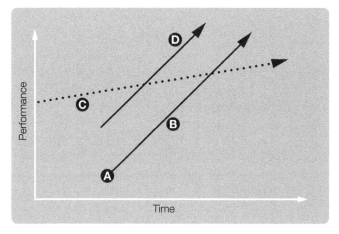

(A) Current performance of potentially disruptive technology

(B) Expected trajectory of performance improvement

(C) Performance improvement required by mainstream market

(D) Expected trajectory of incumbents

Figure 7.6
Performance
Trajectories.
Adapted with
permission of
Harvard Business
Publishing from
Bower and
Christensen (1995).
Copyright ©2005
Harvard Business
Publishing; all rights
reserved.

It may help to think in terms of three types of innovation:

1   Sustaining or incremental innovation is the gradual performance improvement that is evenly distributed across an entire market. It rarely delivers a competitive advantage.

2 Discontinuous or step-change innovation is the kind of dramatic step up in functionality that managers dream of but which rarely happens.

3 Disruptive innovation can provide opportunities to move strategically and "under the radar" of competitors.

The concept of "disrupting yourself before someone else does" has become a common feature of the business lexicon. British Airways launched Go (subsequently floated and then sold to EasyJet); Australian insurer AAMI which was known for its attentive staff and friendly call centre launched online no-frills insurer Bingle; and fashion brands have long operated "diffusion lines" to monetise downmarket versions of themselves. These concepts and others like them are frequently dismissed by management detractors as dangerous distractions. Christensen shows that they are nothing of the sort.

7.6 STRUCTURED CHOICE DECISIONMAKING

Many an organisation finds itself at the end of a thrilling "strategy process" faced with an overwhelming list of options. Sometimes these get filed in the proverbial desk draw. Other times, a decision is made on an opinion or a whim and then a few "compelling reasons" are retrofitted to suit.

Frequently, the larger the spreadsheet, the more confident the organisation becomes about its processes. Numbers convey the illusion of certainty, and managers are routinely hoodwinked by a sophisticated Excel model.

Past success tends to be particularly persuasive in these types of exercise. If we know this is working now, even the most considered analysis might be tempted to downplay the risk of it not working into the future.

To address pitfalls like these, Martin, Rivkin, Siggelkow and Lafley formulated a process which they called Structured Choice Decisionmaking. It aims to define a set of discrete alternatives facing a business and then subject each to a rigorous selection process. Their 2012 Harvard Business Review article[8] contains many gems of good advice summarised in their graphic which we've reproduced in **Figure 7.7**.

A few particular points are worthy of being called out. First, take good care in the way that you set up the process to avoid bland thinking. Start with an explicit choice (*We can do A or B…*) rather than an open-ended "opportunity" or "issue". Then take care to specify the options *in detail*. As we get into the decisionmaking process, the authors remind us to be very explicit about what each option involves. Next, when you define what would be required to make each option work ("the conditions"), be strict about only keeping the essential must-haves in your list. If any condition starts to look like a nice-to-have, interrogate further and be prepared to remove it.

---

8 Lafley, A. G., Martin, R. L., Rivkin, J. W., & Siggelkow, N., 2012, 'Bringing Science to The Art of Strategy', *Harvard Business Review*, Vol. 90, No. 9, pp. 57–66.

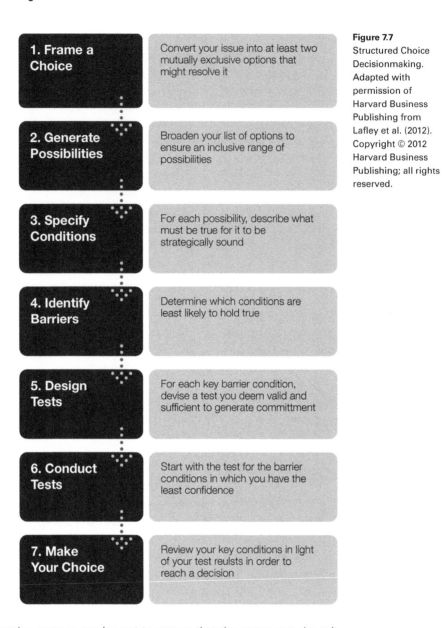

1. Frame a Choice	Convert your issue into at least two mutually exclusive options that might resolve it
2. Generate Possibilities	Broaden your list of options to ensure an inclusive range of possibilities
3. Specify Conditions	For each possibility, describe what must be true for it to be strategically sound
4. Identify Barriers	Determine which conditions are least likely to hold true
5. Design Tests	For each key barrier condition, devise a test you deem valid and sufficient to generate committment
6. Conduct Tests	Start with the test for the barrier conditions in which you have the least confidence
7. Make Your Choice	Review your key conditions in light of your test reuslts in order to reach a decision

Figure 7.7
Structured Choice Decisionmaking. Adapted with permission of Harvard Business Publishing from Lafley et al. (2012). Copyright © 2012 Harvard Business Publishing; all rights reserved.

In any planning process, you've got to ensure that the status quo doesn't get special treatment – either automatically being overvalued as an excellent idea, or being discounted as uninspired or just plain *boring*. In this version, the current strategy is included within the list of alternatives considered to ensure it gets a fair (but firm) hearing.

Martin, Rivkin, Siggelkow and Lafley suggest that you take great care in framing any discussion on potential options:

> If… the dialogue is about what would have to be true, then the sceptic can say, "for me to be confident in this possibility, I would have to know that consumers

will embrace this sort of offering." That is a very different sort of statement from "That will never work!" It helps the proponent understand the sceptic's reservations and develop the proof to overcome them.

Once this is done, a more scientific air descends on the process as we are encouraged to test if these conditions might actually hold true. Many of your tests are likely to be customer-facing ones, designed to yield market intelligence. These might take the form of traditional market research based on declared beliefs or intents (*would you choose this?, what do you value most?*), or a Steve Blank-style test with some form of a prototype. You may also run technical tests (a Proof of Concept) or operate a short production run to ensure the feasibility of a physical process. For further details, jump back to **Model 7.9 Customer Development**.

At the time that the article was published, Lafley had recently retired as CEO of consumer goods giant P&G. The article describes a choice facing P&G: how to capitalise on the market for skincare; a space within which it had one paltry offering: the (then) tired and downmarket brand *Oil of Olay*. The choice was whether to revitalise this brand or to acquire a new one. They explain that one of the conditions required for the revitalisation strategy to work was that consumers would have to be willing to switch from department or speciality stores into discount chemists and supermarkets. So, they undertook market research to establish if this would be possible at a range of price points. The research findings indicated that they would. And the rest, as you probably know, is history.

7.7 STRATEGIC SOUNDNESS

Day's Test of Strategic Soundness provides a structure to validate a possible market-facing strategy. It's a great checklist by which you can assess almost any plan. A strategy that does not meet all five points needs to be reworked or reconsidered.

Our diagram in Figure 7.8 is a heavily summarised version of Day's tests outlined in his book *Market Driven Strategy: Processes for Creating Value*.[9] A slightly different version also appears in *Putting Strategy into Shareholder Value Analysis*, published by Harvard Business Review,[10] also well worth a read.

7.8 SCENARIO PLANNING

A lot of business school alumni will remember that scenario planning was invented by Shell to contemplate the future of the oil price.[11] But what exactly was it?

---

9 Day, G. S., 1990, *Market Driven Strategy: Processes for Creating Value*, The Free Press, New York, pp. 41, 42.

10 Day, G. S., & Fahey, L., 1990, 'Putting Strategy into Shareholder Value Analysis', *Harvard Business Review*, Vol. 68, No. 2, pp. 152–162.

11 Wack, P., February 1985, 'Scenarios: Uncharted Waters Ahead', *Harvard Business Review*, Vol. 91, No. 5, pp. 118–127.

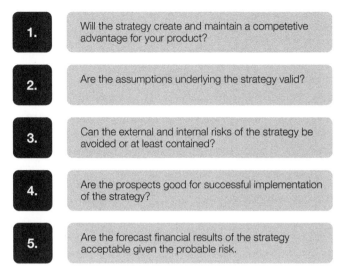

1. Will the strategy create and maintain a competetive advantage for your product?

2. Are the assumptions underlying the strategy valid?

3. Can the external and internal risks of the strategy be avoided or at least contained?

4. Are the prospects good for successful implementation of the strategy?

5. Are the forecast financial results of the strategy acceptable given the probable risk.

Figure 7.8
Day's Test
of Strategic
Soundness. From
*Market Driven
Strategy: Processes
for Creating Value*
by George S. Day.
Copyright © 1990
by George S. Day.
Reprinted with
the permission of
The Free Press, a
division of Simon
& Schuster, Inc. All
rights reserved.

Pierre Wack pointed out that with an infinite number of dependent variables the future was unpredictable, and that as such we should give up on the endless pursuit of an accurate view of the future. The essential principle of scenario planning is about accepting uncertainty. You just don't know what is likely to happen, but you probably do know what the variables are.

Pick two things about which you are unsure. And map their combinations.

Typically, plotting two pairs of opposed alternative futures is used to give four scenarios where each intersects. Typically some of the combinations will be more likely than others, but theoretically, each should be a possible future.

Let's say we are considering the future of something particularly uncertain, like brain-human interfaces implanted in people's heads. Our two axes could be:

- Legal: ranging from complete prohibition to government grants; and
- Provider types: from large corporations providing the service to bio-hackers working on people's heads on their own (or on their own heads!)

The resulting four quadrants throw up scenarios that we might not otherwise have considered, such as commercial operators operating in a world that is technically illegal. Unlikely? Perhaps, but this is of course exactly how many private driver services around the world first became established.

Quadrants like these are useful stimuli for alternative tactics which you might feed into a process like that in **Model 7.6 Structured Choice Decisionmaking**. The potential outcomes also raise issues such as risk (financial or, as in this example, to human health), and how different types of customers or audiences may be affected depending upon how the future plays out.

Figure 7.9
Sample Scenario
Planning Axes.

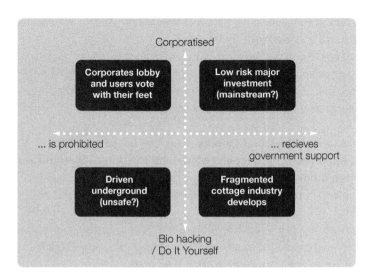

7.9 CUSTOMER DEVELOPMENT

When we first came across Steve Blank's curiously named book *Four Steps to the Epiphany*,[12] it was something of an epiphany itself. And it wouldn't be an exaggeration to say that a lot of our subsequent consulting and product management work was influenced by it.

The *Customer Development* process outlined by Blank in his book turned much of traditional management thinking on its head. It's steeped in pragmatism and might be a little different from the linear frameworks that you came across at business school. It crosses both Strategic Planning and Delivery and as such is probably equally at home in this section of the book and the next one.

At its core, this model has several controversial concepts, such as

- Releasing early – potentially before a product is finished
- Keeping the plan fluid whilst you roll out a new product or feature
- Continuing the research process throughout; and
- Recruiting non-representative participants for research

Although these may make many theoreticians feel uneasy, anyone who was worked with new innovations knows intuitively that these assertions are fundamental truths.

Four Steps to The Epiphany was influential, but it wasn't widely read. It was mainly left to other writers to popularise what Blank had written; most significantly Eric Ries in his book *The Lean Startup*[13] which introduced many readers to the *Minimum Viable Product (or MVP)*, and Dan Olsen's *Lean Product Playbook*[14]

---

12 Blank, S., 2005, *Four Steps to the Epiphany.*
13 Ries, E., 2011, *The Lean Startup.*
14 Olsen, D., 2015, *The Lean Product Playbook.*

which applies similar concepts to new product lines within existing businesses. Steve Blank also maintains an excellent website.[15]

The Four Steps to which it refers are a four-step process to turn innovations into commercial successes. Covering the identification of customers, how they will be approached and how they can be scaled up, the book provides a robust model for bringing new ideas to market and has become something of a bible for start-ups.

The precursors of Customer Development can be seen in **Model 4.1 Core, Actual, Augmented Product** and **Model 4.5 The Job-to-Be-done and Outcome-Driven Innovation**. If the new innovation doesn't actually address a significant problem, then all the business modelling and theorising you do is a waste of time!

The essential principle is to achieve (and prove) that you have product-market fit before committing yourself to a particular direction but to do so without falling into the trap of just asking the customer what they want.

Figure 7.10
The Customer Development Process, based on www.steveblank. com, used with permission.

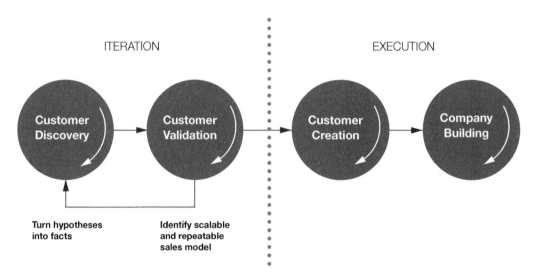

The stages are as follows:[16]

1. Customer Discovery takes the initial idea or insight from the founder or product developer and seeks to unearth customers for whom it might be useful. Customer Discovery isn't about market research as you may have met it before. Far from worrying about the random selection of survey respondents to match the general population, this is a deliberately targeted exercise. It's about speaking to people who you think are likely to be ahead of the rest of the market: people who are already fiddling about with their

---

15 www.steveblank.com.
16 This section draws on a previous article Chris wrote for Mitchel Lake's Digital Pigeon newsletter.

own makeshift solutions to the problem you seek to solve, and people who can provide you with ideas about what the others might want. This isn't Blank's original idea. Several years earlier, Geoffrey Moore described how customers who recognise they have a problem are likely to be those most amenable to your new way of solving it.[17]

2. The next step, Customer Validation, is a stop-and-check stage which adds some commercial overlay to the needs discovered in step one. Its purpose is to determine whether there are sufficient numbers of suitable prospects who you might be able to convert into customers. One outcome of this step is to build a repeatable sales process by answering questions about why and how the right people will buy. Here, Blank introduces us to four types of customers. The awkwardly named earlyvangelists are the ones you want at this point. (This group corresponds to what Eric Von Hippel has termed "Lead Users" – an eminently preferable title.) Early Evaluators are tyre-kickers best avoided, whilst scalable customers and mainstream customers are best left alone for the time being. As has been observed by Geoffrey Moore and others, mainstream customers want to buy the "whole product": a fully functional package rather than something they will need to piece together or configure themselves.

    If Steps 1 and 2 don't yield the desired results, you tweak and repeat until they do; or until you decide on the basis of evidence to abandon the project.

3. Customer Creation is where the traditional growth and sales process takes over. You can refer to **Model 5.4 Blank's Market Types** for more on the key different market dynamics. For an existing market, the primary promotional objective is to take a share from incumbents. In a new market, share is irrelevant ("Therefore spending money on a massive launch to generate customers and market share is ludicrous"). In a re-segmentation situation, the marketing task is both about the share and about re-education; encouraging customers to see themselves and their market in a new way.

4. Company Building is where marketing meets operations. *Four Steps* aims to explain the missing link between successful innovations and successful companies with commentary on company culture (Blank believes companies should progress through a three-stage lifecycle of development-, mission- and process-centricity, reflecting **Model 7.2 The Discipline of Market Leaders**); on decentralisation and hiring; on responses to competitors; and on sales rates.

Yesterday's managers can learn a great deal by embracing the uncertainty and flexibility of Blank's model. But managers steeped in the mindset of Lean Products and MVPs can be susceptible to overreach too.

---

17 Moore, G., 1991, *Crossing the Chasm*, HarperCollins, New York.

Some common mistakes to avoid are:

1. Thinking that everything is a "product". Whilst there *are* times when a new website or brochure may benefit from Customer Development testing and refinement, generally this won't be the case.
2. Losing the power of surprise by testing (and thus signalling) your intent prior to a full launch of a new product or service. The solution here is to test quickly and/or piecemeal (so that the full picture isn't revealed), or within the confines of trusted confidants. Resist the temptation to draw up a lot of glossy-style communication collateral just to support a test – use the power of your own voice and some quick reference documents instead. They are less likely to "leak" as well as take up less of your time.
3. Endless iteration loops that chew up the time and emotional energy of your teams. Be alert to where diminishing returns are setting in! Research isn't a substitute for making decisions.
4. Pivoting instead of parking failed ideas. Some initiatives are best abandoned, but in many businesses, this is hard. One of the important lessons that any business can take from Blank and his disciples is that the organisation should be prepared – or allowed – to fail. If the market tells you there is no product-market fit, sometimes the best thing to do is park rather than pivot. Bank your learnings and move on.

7.10 ETHICAL DECISIONS

Ethics feature in everyday life decisions so it is only fitting that they feature in business decisions too. We'll just cover four ways you can add an ethical barometer to your organisation here:

Values. If your business has established values (see **Model 1.6 Brand Charter and Desired Reputation** or **Model 1.1 Collins' and Porras' Vision Framework**), consider these in onboarding, reviews, how you use data and analytics and in the policies and decisions that you make.

Golden Rule. The principle of assumed reciprocity or treating others as you'd like to be treated is a key tenant in most major religions. Perhaps because of this, some believe it to be the closest we can get to a universal ethical principle.

Grandmother Test. Although we don't know your grandmother, the general view is that your granny is an arbiter of what's decent. Would you be prepared to tell your grandmother what you do at work? If not, then perhaps there's a problem. A common version of this is the Grandchild test – often used to draw out examples of externality (see **Model 2.5 Market Failure**), particularly around pollution and climate change since they are more likely to be around to deal with the mess in future.

Veil of Ignorance Test was articulated by philosopher John Rawls in the 1970s. The test – which Rawls used to establish "principles of justice" but which can also be used on just about any decision of consequence – concerns whether *without knowing one's circumstances in society* one would choose a particular outcome. Imagine you were ignorant of your own gender, race, age, place of birth and so on – a disembodied mind yet to occupy a body – would you choose this same course of action?

8 Delivery

How we ensure arrival

It's frequently observed that the so-called Strategy Consultancies make more revenue from coordinating implementation than they do from deciding upon a strategy in the first place. This shouldn't be surprising: delivery takes more work – and it's typically done by more people.

In this section, we aim to show several models that might help you. Many of these you probably wouldn't meet at business school, where the formulation of strategy – rather than its implementation – is frequently the focus.

Your aim in *Delivery* is to achieve the much-lauded (but rarely seen) concept of an organisation-wide commitment to achieving the desired market outcome.

WHAT TO LOOK OUT FOR

We observed earlier that success is not a state of mind. Neither is it a slide deck. Delivery is the point where choosing A over B means actually ceasing B and starting A!

You'll be judged by what you do more than what you say. Watch out for a strategy that stops short of delivery, or one that is vague and inconclusive or a strategy that is isolated from the rest of the organisation.

Theory is easy because those are just words on a page or whiteboard. Humans on the other hand are inherently messy. They have opinions, egos, feelings of loss or trepidation in the face of change. Ignore this at your peril!

Sadly, there's no silver bullet for delivery. But it gets a lot easier for people to follow when there are clear outcomes, clear structure and clear objectives. And when people are involved in the formulation of the plan, generally engagement will be higher.

DOI: 10.4324/9781003038276-8

It's sometimes said that a B-grade strategy with an A-grade execution is preferable to an A-grade strategy with a B-grade execution. But this is not reflected in how many businesses choose to spend their time. And how often do we see a delivery decision made without reference to the strategy?

Is what you do in alignment with what you say you'll do? Indeliberate acts – accidental ways of working – can cloud the message and will undermine confidence in the strategy.

8.1 GOALS VERSUS STRATEGY VERSUS TACTICS

What's a strategy? What's a goal? What's a tactic? What's the difference? One of the challenges of modern strategy is that it has no accepted, commonly understood languages like accounting or engineering. Sure, you will find countless texts that provide endless definitions, but they are so often contradictory and confusing – what one calls a "vision", another calls a "mission", one company's plan is another's strategy and so on.

We won't solve that problem here, but we do have a view that there are two essential attributes of successful implementation of strategic plans:

1. The language you use is consistently understood and applied within your organisation.
2. There are clear links between long-term ambitions, mid-term strategies and shorter-term plans.

Think of it in terms of cascading time horizons with longer-term "big picture" stuff at the top increasingly tactical elements as you go down into the detail.

It's a good working principle that goals should be SMART – that is specific, measurable, actionable, realistic and time-bound. (OK, so there's some overlap in there, but it's the best mnemonic we know.)

How long is long-term and how short is short-term is likely to be driven by the industry in which you operate. If you are in a web-technology business, then long-term might be three years or less. If you are in biotech, long-term might be five years or more.

The choice of tools is up to you – and you are likely to be best served by designing your own. We've included a few in this section. The trick in our view is to achieve alignment across everyone within the firm.

Before we get onto planning frameworks we'll stop to visit two assessment models: the Balanced Scorecard and the Objectives and Key Results (OKR).

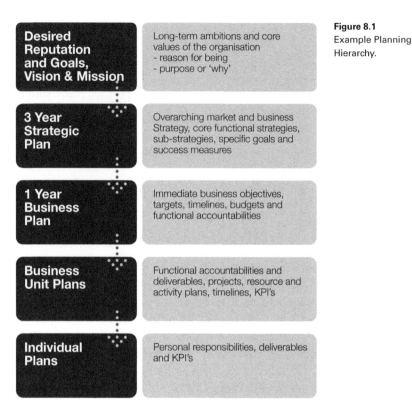

Figure 8.1
Example Planning
Hierarchy.

8.2 BALANCED SCORECARD

The Balanced Scorecard is usually associated with Kaplan and Norton who we previously met in **Model 7.2 The Discipline of Market Leaders**. Kaplan and Norton's scorecard[1] was "balanced" because it had four elements or "perspectives" – financial, internal business capability, innovation and learning and customer (Figure 8.2).

To today's eyes, it seems self-evident that the purpose of a business is not just to make money, but in 1992, it was revolutionary. This is reminiscent of "triple bottom line accounting" (now known as environmental and social goals or "ESG") – which considers social and environmental as well as direct financial outcomes – also a product of the mid-1990s.

It's easy to see how the customer perspective links to many of the other theories that we have been discussing. If you want a refresher, try jumping back to models for customer analysis (Chapter 4).

The financial one is easy to understand.

The internal business perspective and to a lesser extent the innovation and learning perspective cover the capabilities – or competences – that the organisation commits to pursuing. We met these in **Model 3.1 Capabilities and Core Competences**.

---

1 Kaplan, R., & Norton, D., January–February 1992, 'The Balanced Scorecard – Measures That Drive Performance', *Harvard Business Review*, Vol. 70, pp. 71–79.

Like many of the other models that we cover, they also highlight the difference between goals and measures. A goal, for the uninitiated, might be "become the most famous plumbers' merchant in USA", while the metric could be "achieve 70% unprompted awareness". The goal is easy to understand, while the metric is unequivocal, and hard to wriggle out of. We'll come back to this in **Model 8.3 OKRs**.

It's really hard to put values into a Key Performance Indicator (KPI) framework. But one way is through the lens of reputational assessment – to what effect do customers or other stakeholders agree that your organisation displays particular behaviours or principles?

The Balanced Scorecard
Links Performance Measures

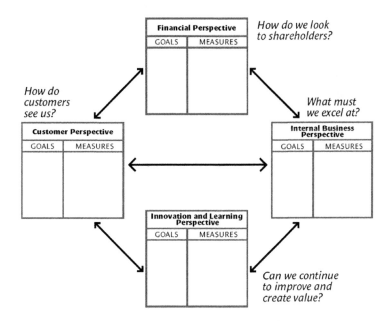

Figure 8.2
Kaplan and Norton's Balanced Scorecard. Reproduced with permission of Harvard Business Publishing from Kaplan and Norton (1992), Copyright © 1992 Harvard Business Publishing; all rights reserved.

8.3 OKRs

Outcomes and Key Results are a useful way of framing what you are supposed to be doing. Then again, so are KPIs (Key Performance Indicators if you've forgotten) and plain old goals.

Years ago, we would run workshops where execs would enthuse about "profitability" being a goal. This may be strictly speaking correct. But it generally doesn't motivate anyone other than the shareholders. It's also somewhat soulless, and it doesn't tell you much about how you're going to do it.

We said before that goals should be specific. That's the principle behind the OKR. The O stands for Objective, while the KR stands for Key Results – as in "*what key results will show that we've met the objective?*". In totality, OKRs should answer this question. John Doerr introduced the world to OKRs in his book

Measure What Matters,[2] and his website gives some examples from Google and others.

OKRs – or any other kind of very specific goals – come into their own when managers are faced with competing priorities. *How do I choose between A and B, if I can only do one of them?* The answer is, you choose the action which you expect to either contribute to the *greatest number of OKRs* or *drive the highest performance of a particular OKR*. Which of these you choose will depend upon your business, and how you've characterised your objectives.

Doerr frequently deploys a set of KRs with a single objective, and in this way, his approach often looks rather like a set of coordinated initiatives that will together achieve a particular outcome. Back to Rumelt's coordinated activities, or (as we will see in a moment) to SOSTAC's tactics and actions.

8.4 SOSTAC

This is the first planning framework that we'll cover, but there are several to choose from, and the right one depends upon you and your circumstances.

The SOSTAC framework was created by PR Smith in the 1990s.[3] It was conceived mainly as a marketing planning tool – but one with plenty of application beyond the marketing department which is why it's included here.

The six elements of the framework are

- Situation
- Objectives
- Strategy
- Tactics
- Action
- Control

Situation is our *Analysis* (see Chapters 2–6). You are likely to find it especially valuable if you can articulate challenges that have to be addressed using frameworks such as **Model 2.3 The Value Chain** or **Model 6.3 The Value Net**.

To add some "why" to the objectives, you could use Collins and Porras (**Model 1.1**); perhaps supplemented with values from a Brand Charter (**Model 1.6**);

Strategy is much of what this book is about.

Tactics could be identified using any of the tools in Chapter 7, such as **Models 7.5 Disruptive Innovation**, **7.2 The Discipline of Market Leaders** or **7.8 Scenario Planning**.

Finally, Control refers to the need to react, reassess and adjust based on market feedback. For this, you might use the metrics we met from Kaplan and Norton's Balanced Scorecard (**Model 8.2**) or OKRs (**Model 8.3**).

---

2 Doerr, J., 2017, *Measure What Matters*, New York.
3 www.SOSTAC.org.

SOSTAC isn't unique – a point that PR Smith himself points out – but it is a great way of thinking about your plan. What is common to all good planning frameworks is that they feature some element of outlining a future scenario and breaking down the steps required to get there. Something that is sometimes clumsily referred to as "back-casting".

You'll also see some of the same themes from earlier pop up again – there's a diagnosis, a guiding vision and a set of reinforcing actions. Think back to the start of this book and they appear in **Model 1.2 Kernel of Strategy**.

8.5 MARKET-BASED STRATEGY FRAMEWORK™

This is the only tool in this book that is ours. That said, only the act of combining these concepts on one page is new: it draws on several of the well-regarded frameworks outlined in this book. It seeks to achieve alignment between reputation, ambition, the market and the organisation (Figure 8.3).

There was a time when Grant would be developing a Market-Based Strategy for a different client every couple of weeks, and many organisations across Australia and New Zealand benefited from using this framework to organise themselves and align themselves around a common set of objectives. You'll recognise some of the other elements from this book, but we're not particular about which to use. Choose the model that works for you – or change it to suit your circumstances. But *do have a plan*. As the old saying goes, "a strategy without a plan is a plan to fail".

The key principles are

* Link the strategy back to the market: your customers
* Keep it very tight: if you can, go for four values or less, between six and ten pathways, and goals that the average person can understand in a couple of minutes

Regardless of the model you use, remember to leave room for iteration. As we saw in **Model 7.9 Customer Development**, achieving that elusive fit between customers and your organisation is critical. Don't create a plan that locks you in so much that you can't allow an appropriate degree of evolution or responsiveness to the market.

8.6 BUSINESS MODEL CANVAS (BMC)

Rarely has one model been as rapidly adopted as the Business Model Canvas, created in 2005 and popularised in a book of the same name by Osterwalder et al.[4]

The BMC is a handy way to encapsulate all of the key decisions and policies of a business (but probably not its strategy) on a single page. The three boxes on the left relate to what happens upstream or within the organisation, while

4 Osterwalder, A., 2010, *Business Model Generation: A Handbook for Visionaries, Game Changers, and Challengers*, Wiley, Hoboken.

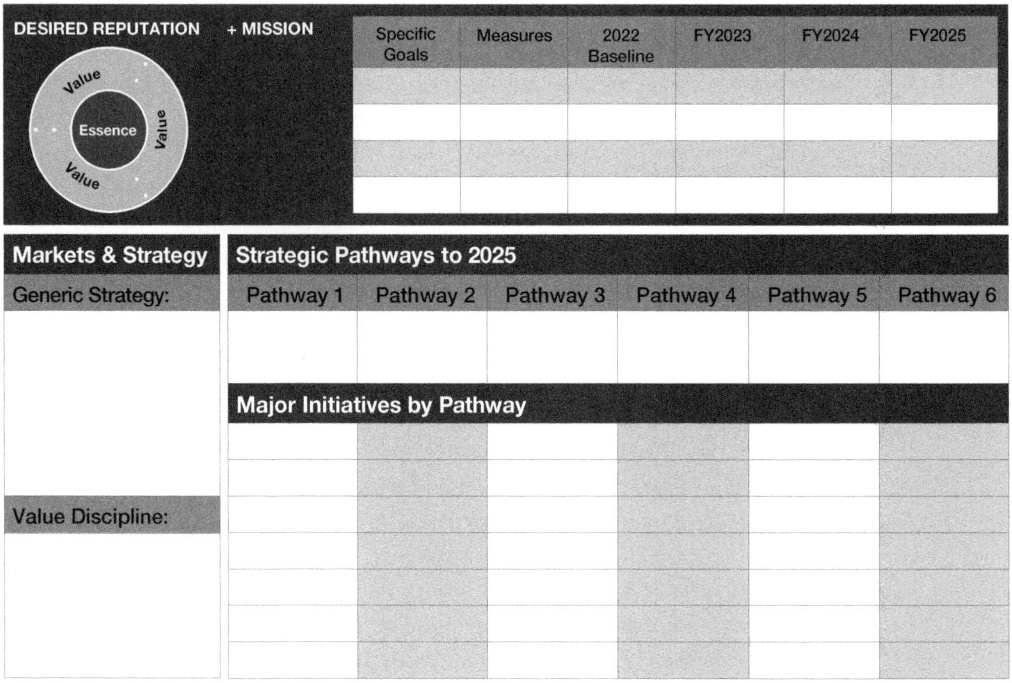

DESIRED REPUTATION + MISSION	Specific Goals	Measures	2022 Baseline	FY2023	FY2024	FY2025
Value / Essence / Value / Value						

Markets & Strategy	Strategic Pathways to 2025					
Generic Strategy:	Pathway 1	Pathway 2	Pathway 3	Pathway 4	Pathway 5	Pathway 6
	Major Initiatives by Pathway					
Value Discipline:						

the three on the right are what happens downstream. The middle box ("Value Propositions") is the intersection of company and market.

It *looks* simple enough. But doing a proper job of filling out the BMC should take time. For instance, under "Customer Segments", don't fall back on the generic ("Shoppers", "B2B Clients") but give as much detail as you can. And then connect the boxes – what proposition will resonate with which particular segment and what key activities and key resources will be necessary to bring it to life? If necessary, use a different BMC for each division or market.

The BMC (which is published under a Creative Commons licence) is here reproduced in full, but we recommend visiting the Strategyzer website to download a copy if you want to use it.[5]

Figure 8.3
Market-Based Strategy Framework.

8.7 AGILE DELIVERY

Agile isn't really a model – it's more of a philosophy or approach. It's become such a buzzword since we started thinking about this book that we couldn't really skip over it. Especially where your business is concerned with software (and *what isn't* these days?).

Often when people say "agile" they really just mean "nimble"; as in, *we make decisions quickly round here*, or *we can pull a team together in half an hour*. But to project managers and software engineers, agile has a precise set of meanings and principles.

---

5 https://www.strategyzer.com/canvas/business-model-canvas.

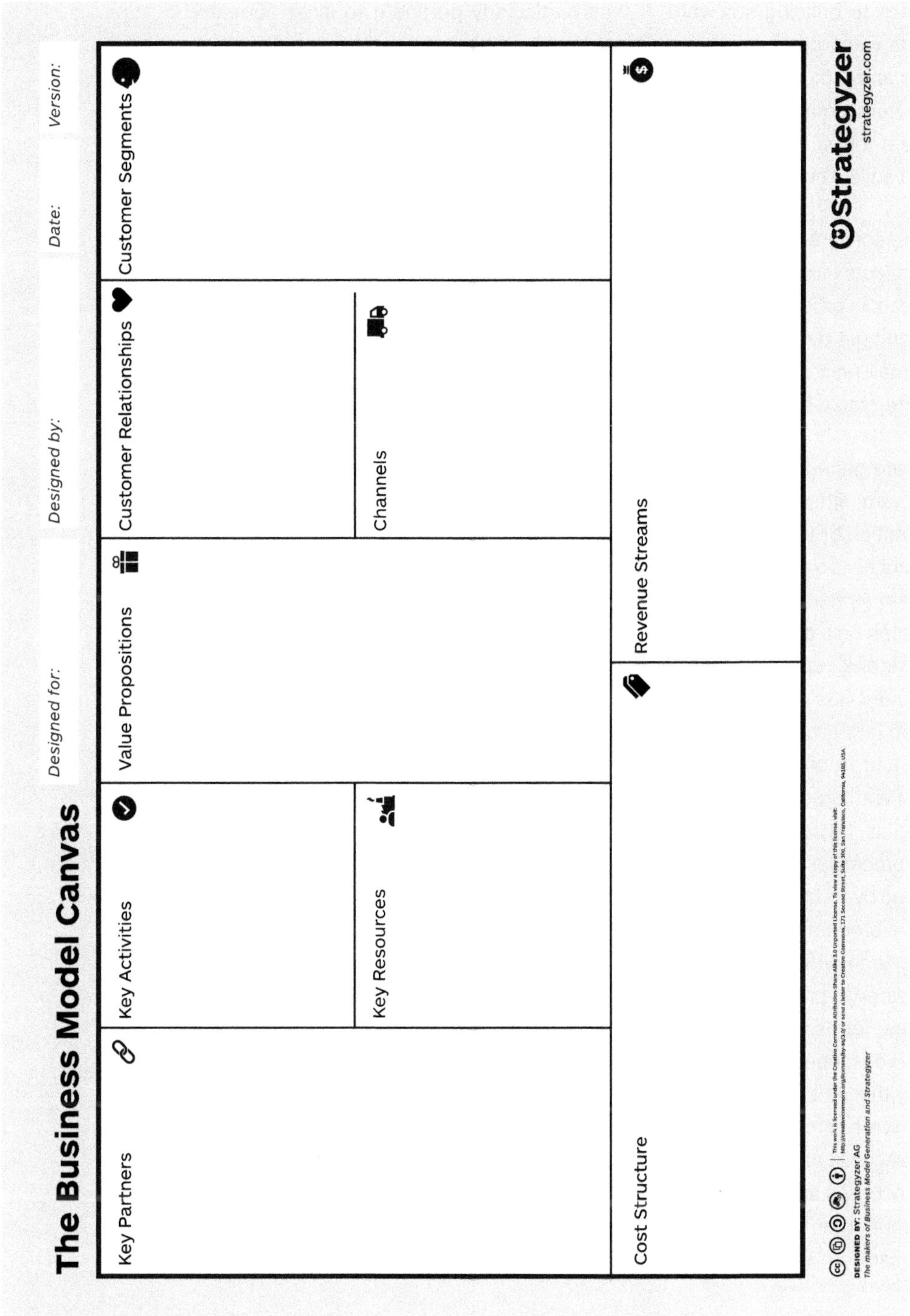
The Business Model Canvas
Designed for:
Designed by:
Date:
Version:
Key Partners
Key Activities
Key Resources
Value Propositions
Customer Relationships
Channels
Customer Segments
Cost Structure
Revenue Streams
DESIGNED BY: Strategyzer AG
The makers of Business Model Generation and Strategyzer
Strategyzer
strategyzer.com

Figure 8.4
Business Model Canvas. Creative Commons Licence.

This meaning of agile goes back to the Agile Manifesto[6] which was published in 2001 as a response to what its authors felt was an overly bureaucratic approach to building software. It was particularly pertinent to large complex projects with lots of unknowns. The Agile Manifesto's focus on human contact, testing and prototyping seems fairly commonplace today but two decades ago it was truly remarkable.

Fast-forward to today where there is a whole industry and vocabulary around agile. There are many variants but a few principles are fairly consistent:

- Projects are broken down into small (sometimes *very* small) tasks
- Projects can start before the whole project is specified
- Work in progress (WIP) is kept to a minimum so that those involved in tasks don't get overwhelmed or rendered inefficient by jumping between tasks
- Small teams are assigned to work on the small tasks – these teams are often multi-disciplinary; for example, designers working with engineers

There are generally considered to be two main ways to practice agile: Kanban and Scrum; although in reality most businesses that practice agile operate in a combination of the two, sometimes known as Scrumban.

Kanban is a Japanese word for a process originally developed by Taiichi Ohno at Toyota as part of its just-in-time manufacturing approach. At its core, tasks are placed on a board with the next up at the top; the engineer or assembly-line operator picks up the next task when they are ready to perform it.

Scrum has many of the same elements of Kanban, except that work is planned into time blocks, known as sprints. Work is estimated upfront so that the outcome of the sprint can be known in advance. Sprints give a team a rhythm with predictable milestones of briefing, celebration and review sessions (known as "retrospectives" or "retros"). Another idea from Toyota's manufacturing processes – Kaisen – which refers to continuous improvement, has been co-opted by today's agile practitioners where team members are encouraged to improve productivity and performance with each successive sprint.

Agile in all its forms is frequently contrasted in none-too-glowing terms with Waterfall project management – as if the two were mortally opposed. We disagree. Terms like Agifall (which sounds better than Watergile) are sometimes used to describe what reality is more like: a set of high-level time-bound objectives within which a series of iterative cycles can take place.

If we had one criticism, it is that Agile has become its own orthodoxy. Ironically Agile has become somewhat un-nimble in many organisations as rigorous processes and strict, multi-layered procedures govern how things are done and real human interaction – with its messy unpredictable nature – starts to disappear from view. It's worth remembering that the Agile Manifesto asked us

6 www.agilemanifesto.org.

to reflect on the messy, human state of the world rather than a didactic overly structured way of working.

One thing is clear – in an uncertain world, don't waste time. Make a decision, and move fast. You can always change direction later.

8.8 PITCH FRAMEWORK

If you've come up with a plan or a strategy – whether for a business or for a product or initiative – it's likely at some point that you'll need to sell it.

We've also used pitching as a way of focusing a team – for example, at the end of a rapid ideation programme.

There's an endless stream of clickbait posts about pitching. And the truth is that there is no one solution. But we have found that most successful pitches include at the very least the following elements:

- **Problem** – why are we here?
- **Solution** – how will we solve the problem?
- **Business Model** – how will this product / service / feature be delivered and paid for?
- **Market Opportunity** – how much scope is there to fix this issue?

Figure 8.5
A Typical Kanban Board.

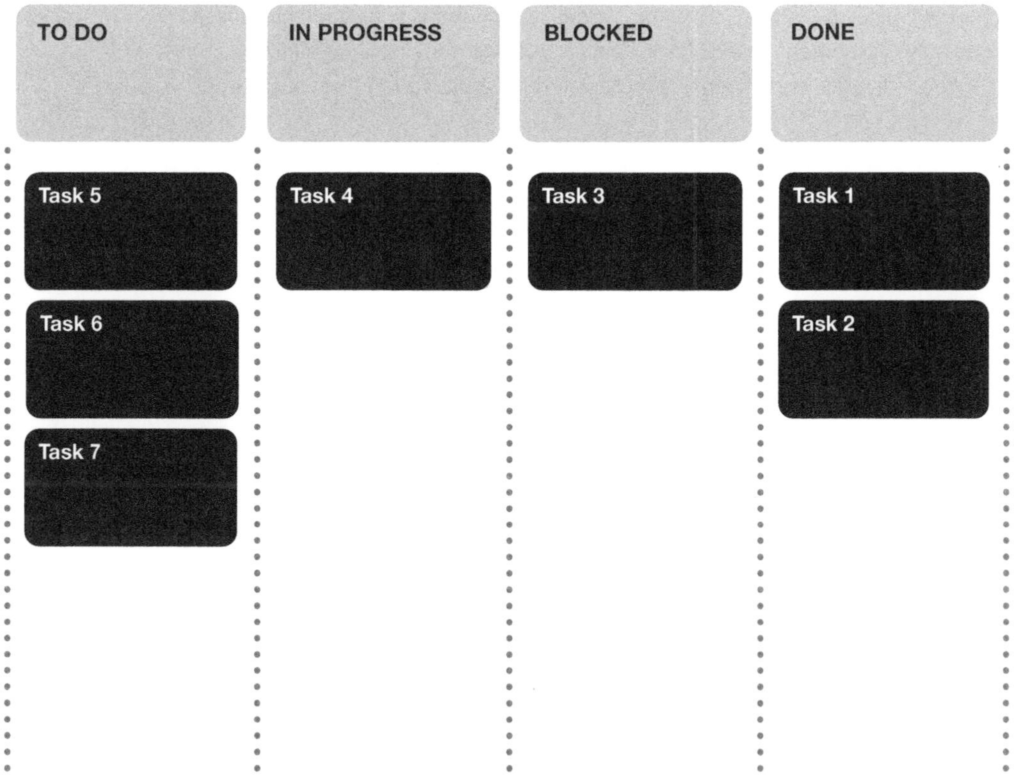

- **Credibility** – why are we the team / company / department to do this?
- **Competition** – who else is doing this?
- **Competitive Advantage** – why is ours going to be different / better?
- **The Ask** – please support this, advocate for us, or fund it!

You probably won't go too far wrong if you refer to David Beckett's "Best 3 Minutes" Pitch Canvas which we have reproduced on the next page. Like the BMC, the Best 3 Minutes Pitch Canvas is also helpfully available under a Creative Commons licence. We suggest you download a copy if you want to use it.[7]

8.9 ROGEN PRESENTATION FRAMEWORK

As for how you present your arguments – whether in a formal "pitch" or indeed any presentation – there is no absolute right answer, but one tool worth thinking about is the Rogen Presentation framework. Actor Peter Rogen established his presentation training firm many years ago (now owned by TTech) which has helped craft many successful pitches over the years.

The basic Rogen framework is shown in **Figure 8.7**. It opens with two general points of summary (this is one of those rare cases where the What *does* come before the Why), before moving into the detail. Each point of your presentation can be summarised with a Key Message that is followed by Evidence and a Takeaway.

The Takeaway is the "so what…". Ideally, you want your audience to be nodding in agreement as you finish this part so that they have little choice but to agree with your overall conclusion as you tie everything together at the end.

---

7 www.Best3Minutes.com.

The Pitch Canvas©

An entrepreneurial brainstorming tool that helps you structure and visualise your pitch on one page

Simple Statement of what change you and your product are making in the world.

A memorable one-sentence explanation of what you do for customers.

Pain (+ Gain)

What problem are you solving for your customers?
What does the pain result in?
Can you make the pain a human problem, that everyone can relate to?
How many people need this problem solved – market size?
Have you validated that people will pay to have it solved?

Product

As simply as possible: How does it work?
What does your product do for customers?
What can your customers do as a result of your product?
What opportunities do you provide for people to be faster, more cost-effective, more efficient, happier, safer?
How have you tested it with customers?
(Be sure not to let the product dominate the pitch.)

Product Demo

Live demo? (always risky, but powerful if it works...)
A screenflow movie of a working App convinces this is for real. Physical product convinces you can execute.
Screenshots are also OK, but can look like a mock-up – moving product on screen is better.
Can you show a real customer using it?

What's Unique

Technology/Relationships/Partnerships.
How do you help your customers get results differently to your competition, or alternatives?
What's new and innovative about your solution?
Show you have researched the market and know what competition is out there.

Customer Traction

Success so far?
Pilot customers? Major brands?
Progression in users or downloads?
Customer reference quotes or movies?
PR coverage? Competition wins?
Use data and facts to strengthen your case.

Business Model

How do you get paid?
What's the opportunity for growth?
How can you scale beyond your current scope: new industries, territories, applications of partnerships and technology?

Investment

Have you invested money yourself?
Have you raised money so far?
How much are you looking for now?
What big next steps will you use the investment for?
What milestones will you reach with the money?
How many, and what type of investor are you looking for?
What expectations do you have of your investors; network, expertise?

Team

What relevant experience and skills does your team have that supports your story?
Brands worked for? Achievements? Sales success?
What binds you together as people and as entrepreneurs to fix this problem?
What's special about the character of your team, that will make you stand out and be memorable?

Call To Action and End Statement

Finish the pitch strongly with a clear request for the audience to take action – what is their first next step?

Why You?

NOTE: Why You? can show up in any part of the pitch.
Why do you care about solving this problem for your customers? How has your life been affected by this industry?
Why should your audience have confidence that you are driven to do what you promise, no matter what?

Figure 8.6
The Best 3 Minutes Pitch Canvas. Creative Commons Licence.

■ Delivery

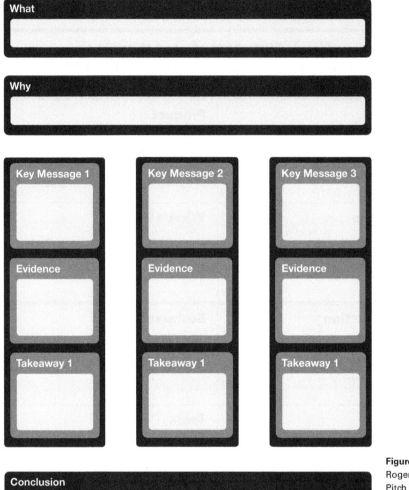

What

Why

Key Message 1

Evidence

Takeaway 1

Key Message 2

Evidence

Takeaway 1

Key Message 3

Evidence

Takeaway 1

Conclusion

Figure 8.7
RogenSI/TTEC
Pitch Framework,
Copyright ©TTEC
2000, used with
Permission.

9   Bringing It All Together

The single most important message that we hope you take away from this book is the *interconnectedness of good strategy*. Models or frameworks used in isolation rarely move the organisation forward and can in fact damage the little cohesion that exists naturally among a group of people.

The better approach is to look for connections – engender them, strive for them. First, between frameworks that you use, and second, between the strategic or "innovation" realm and so-called "business as usual". Deliberately link the decisions that you make to the way that your business operates.

There are many famous examples of organisations that do this well, and business schools are full of case studies. 3M – known for its culture of innovation – has designed processes and policies that engender and reward innovation (and don't punish failure). For many years, Toyota was focused on continuous improvement and new technology – spurred on by pride in proving to a sceptical world that a Japanese brand could outsmart the very best European automotive marques. Consistent with this, its overriding value discipline was *Operational Excellence*. Ryanair didn't become Europe's biggest airline without being ruthlessly focused on cutting unnecessary costs at every turn, choosing to stick to *Actual rather than Augmented* in its product offering. But case studies like these are often hard for younger, smaller or less-famous businesses to relate to – so it boils down to this: think about your own organisation: is the strategy clear? And is the business coherent?

If you wanted to cause irritation in your ranks, you would cherry-pick a few frameworks for a quarantined workshop where everyone goes back to what they were doing the day afterwards. Diagnosis – where we start from – is frequently ignored, as a business acts like it is further evolved than the management team have just agreed it is. Mission and Values, as we noted at the start of this book, are frequently interpreted as cosmetic exercises. Similarly, SWOT often gets rolled out at a management offsite (never to be seen again), while elements of Challenger Brands or Generic Strategies pop up on a PowerPoint for the executive team but aren't actually driven down through the business. This gives strategy a bad name and, as Richard Rumelt would say, is an exercise in "business buzz speak".

DOI: 10.4324/9781003038276-9

We would prefer that you use the frameworks in this book to illuminate and structure a coherent narrative for your organisation. Take the particular case of Vision and Values (what we called Brand Charter in **Model 1.6**). Is this reflected in the decisions that the organisation makes? Does it really "live the values"? Similarly, regarding Value Disciplines (**Model 7.2**), or Porter's Generic Strategies (**Model 7.1**) – taken together and working together, these will provide a powerful foundation for a mutually reinforcing focus that resonates with employees and customers alike. If you've chosen to be "operationally excellent", are you really acting this way? Or are there parts of the business that behave as if "product leadership" was the chosen direction? If the organisation has determined that advantage will come from investment in the supply chain, or demand forecasting then is that investment forthcoming? If you used the Favourable Point of Difference from Value Propositions in B2B Markets (**Model 4.4**) or the ERRC Grid from Blue Ocean Strategy (**Model 7.3**) and decided to differentiate by reducing wastage for customers, are you actually doing this or not? There's always room for aspiration – but ultimately this is a time for self-reflection and brutal honesty.

If strategy is to mean anything at all, it must be reflected in everything that the organisation does. Separating strategy from everything else the company does is an artificial – and deeply unhelpful – mistake. *What* might indeed come before *How*. But the two are intertwined; so much so that one is tempted to wonder if, in some way, delivery *is* strategy.

Let's stop for a moment and consider four key reasons why alignment is important.[1]

First, with alignment, companies don't need to build an entire ecosystem for every new product or new client. A degree of commonality in how a business goes about its work leads to efficiency and effectiveness. As we saw in **Model 5.2**, the so-called "experience curve" enables organisations to get better at particular tasks by doing them more than once. Companies that are aligned have lower marginal costs than equivalent companies that are not.

Second, alignment is the only way of influencing reputation for the better. Organisations need a demonstrable track record of a particular type of behaviour for a particular perception to stick – a single great event alone won't do it. **Model 4.21** looked at how reputations are worth building: they open doors, reduce acquisition costs and increase retention rates.

Third, Alignment means adherence to a consistent way of working – a necessary ingredient in creating cultural cohesion in the workplace. This is important if you want people to collaborate successfully and enjoy working together.

Fourth, Alignment is essential to the execution of strategy. Since strategy is about committing to a particular course of action (and saying "no" to others), the ability to follow through – across a business and over time – is essential. Given that a company can't do everything, coordinated decisions and continued

---

1 This section draws on Chris's 2010 article for Nine/Fairfax media: *Alignment is about getting all your little ducks in a row.*

focus are critical. Do you know in which parts of your business you should pursue innovation, and where maintenance or parity is OK?

In one particular example, a leading home and automotive insurer systematically worked through Purpose, Vision, Mission, Generic Strategies, Value Disciplines and landed on Core Competences. This provided an unprecedented degree of focus and consistency but did not shut out innovation. Decisionmaking was as close to the customer as possible – but new ideas and initiatives had to sit between the guardrails provided by the strategy. In this way, rather than limiting the ability to make decisions, the organisation was able to empower its team and stay true to its chosen direction without creating an unfocussed splurge of wasted energy. The company used its tight grasp on strategy to good effect to decide what not to do. At one stage it found that – because of its commitment to peace of mind for customers – it was facilitating car rentals from a well-known provider based within its service centres. *Why not enter the car rental market?* A clear strategy made answering this question easy. Becoming a car rental company would not fit with the capabilities of the organisation; it was not aligned to the chosen Value Disciplines; and it didn't support the brand. The decision to partner rather than insource or acquire was simple, and the business remained focused.

Life is easier when people move in step. "People are our biggest asset" is an often-heard claim. And while accountants might wince (people aren't strictly assets), for a lot of businesses, the sentiment is true. Engaging people is always important and frequently critical; particularly where discretionary effort has a large role to play – and that's pretty much any product business, services company or not-for-profit, plus many others. If you want people to make decisions (rather than make decisions for them) you need to give them a map. Your strategy, if consistently well-articulated, can help you do this.

The challenge grows when the organisation grows. Very small companies are frequently quite focused naturally – there are only a few staff and they are united by a clear common goal (it may be why they formed together in the first place). But without effort, this uniformity of purpose fades away as an organisation grows. Good leadership will create the right balance between ensuring that the strategy is up-to-date and unsettling the team by creating the impression of a constant state of flux or indecision.

Our last diagram – *The Marketing Mix* – is another favourite of marketers, but we think it has resonance across all and every part of an organisation. Philip Kotler used to talk about the "Five Ps" of marketing. At some point, this increased to the seven Ps, then eight, and we've even heard of nine or more. We think that we've shown enough to adequately make the point: your strategy is manifest through what you do, not what you say. Our version, true to the customer-centric roots of the model, shows the brand strategy at the top. But the principle holds true for The Hedgehog Concept, the 7-S, or Blank's Market Types, or pretty much anything else in this book. Strategy is for living, not just for presenting.

If there's one word that sums up what can give your organisation the edge, it's **alignment**. Alignment is the one word that touches upon *all* of the models in this book. It's the glue that ultimately holds everything together. Alignment across the business, and alignment between the business, its marketplace, and its customers.

And remember, hoping for success is not a strategy. Good luck.

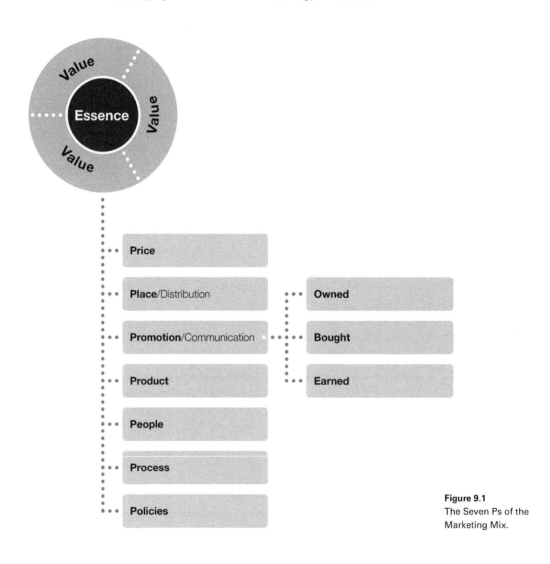

Figure 9.1
The Seven Ps of the Marketing Mix.

Appendix

A.1 RESOURCES

Originality was not our aim in writing this book. If anything is new about it, then we hope it's the way that we've helped you navigate around the range of excellent frameworks, concepts and ideas that others have developed but few have interrelated.

The accompanying website provides links to all the source references and suggested further reading – organised in the same way as the book.

www.essentialmanagementmodels.com

"Hope is not a strategy"

A.2 ABOUT

Grant and Chris worked together for many years across several companies, starting with Swat Marketing in Melbourne, Australia. This book evolved out of a large file of models and commentary that we built whilst working together and beyond.

Grant ran his market strategy consulting business Ellis Foster McVeigh from 2009 to 2019 during which time he created more shareholder value and social impact than most consultants would in a lifetime. A highly sought-after educator in Melbourne, Sydney and Hong Kong, Grant had held adjunct lecturer posts with Macquarie Graduate School of Management, the Graduate School of Business at the University of Sydney, Mt Eliza Business School (now Melbourne Business School) and the Australian Graduate School of Management. Grant was a member of the Australian Institute of Company Directors and also a director of crisis support charity Lifeline Australia. Prior to his consulting career, Grant was GM of Marketing and Sales for business telco Commander Australia. He had an MBA from Bond University. Grant passed away in 2019.

Chris has held several roles in strategy, innovation, product development and related areas. He is Chief Product Officer for education marketplace Adventus. io. He advises several early-stage businesses and has held senior positions at Carsales.com and Solvup.com/TIC Group after working with Grant as marketing and strategy business consultant. He has an MBA from Melbourne Business School. Chris has written for the *Financial Times, WARC/Market Leader, Nine/Fairfax* and others.

This book is not a guide to the businesses, past or present, that Grant or Chris have worked with or advised. *Essential Management Models* represents the authors' personal opinions.

A.3 THANKS

Many of the models included in this book were suggested by colleagues and teachers past and present. Jon "the Pricing Prophet" Manning provided thoughts, feedback and detailed recommendations. Our former client Robert Belleville provided much of the reading list, gave very considered input and constantly reminded us of the importance of alignment. Associate Professor Kwangui Lim from Melbourne Business School kindly provided detailed recommendations on the structure of the manuscript.

For particular sections, thanks to Professor Susan Ellis for suggestions in Product Lifecycle and Day's Test of Strategic Soundness, and to Dr Catherine de Fontenay for a refresher on economic theory. I'm grateful to David Roth at WPP, Michael Sussman at BAV Group and Graham Staplehurst at Kantar for assistance with examples and content. Mark Ritson, Michael Cameron and Tony Ulwick, cheers! David Fox, the cover rocks.

In addition to the above, thanks for proofreading, encouragement and other suggestions from Julia Lipski, Richard Uren, Amanda Heyworth, Samantha Hellams, and my parents Mike and Kathryn Grannell.

To Lorraine Foster for helping the book to happen. To my family Louise, Stella, Aiden and Hamish for allowing me to spend countless weekends and evenings re-writing and chasing up permissions. To all at Routledge: Amy Laurens for seeing the potential; and Rebecca Marsh, Katie Hemmings and Lauren Whelan for bringing it to life. Thank you.

Thanks to Quentin and Scotty at Canyon Brand for many of the original graphics – a few have been tweaked, extended or adapted so thanks for letting me do that. (If there's any jankiness introduced to the illustrations, the fault lies with me.) With Mark you created a wonderful working environment for us where Grant and I laid down the skeleton of this book back in 2009–2010.

Most of all the eternal gratitude of a co-author goes to Grant Foster to whom this book is dedicated.

CJG, April 2022

Bibliography

Aaker, D. A., 1996, *Building Strong Brands*, Free Press, New York.

Aaker, D. A., & Joachminsthaler, E. A., 2000, 'The Brand Relationship Spectrum: The Key to the Brand Architecture Challenge', *California Management Review*, Vol. 42, No. 4, pp. 8–23.

Anderson, C., 2006, *The Long Tail*, Hyperion, New York.

Anderson, J. C., Narus, J. A., & Van Rossum, W., 2006, 'Customer Value Propositions in Business Markets', *Harvard Business Review*, Vol. 84, pp. 91–99.

Ansoff, H., September–October 1957, 'Strategies for Diversification', *Harvard Business Review*, pp. 113–124.

Baghai, M., Coley, S., & White, D., 1999, *The Alchemy of Growth*, Orion Publishing, London.

Benkard, L., 2000, 'Learning and Forgetting: The Dynamics of Aircraft Production', *American Economic Review*, Vol. 90, No. 4, pp. 1034–1054.

Blank, S., 2005, *Four Steps to the Epiphany*, Café Press, San Mateo, CA.

Bower, J. L., & Christensen, C. M., February 1995, 'Disruptive Technologies Catching the Wave', *Harvard Business Review*, Vol. 73, pp. 43–53.

Brandenburger, A. M., & Nalebuff, B. J., 1996, *Co-opetition*, Double Day, New York.

Cardwell, G., 1972, *Turning Points in Western Technology; A Study of Technology, Science and History*, Science History Publishing, New York.

Chaffey, D., Ellis-Chadwick, F., Johnstone, K., & Mayer, R., 2008, *Internet Marketing: Strategy, Implementation and Practice*, 4th edn, FT Prentice Hall, London.

Christensen, C., et al., September 2016, 'Know Your Customers' "Jobs to Be Done"', *Harvard Business Review*, Vol. 94, No. 9, pp. 54–62.

Claessens, M., 2015, Product Lifecycle Strategies (PLC) and Characteristics – Managing Each PLC Stage, Marketing Insider, https://marketing-insider.eu/product-life-cycle-strategies/

Collins, J., 2006, *Good to Great*, Random House, London.

Coyne, K. P., Hall, S. J. D., & Clifford, P. G., 1997, 'Is Your Core Competence a Mirage?', *McKinsey Quarterly*, Vol. 1, pp. 40–54.

Day, G. S., 1990, *Market Driven Strategy: Processes for Creating Value*, Free Press, a division of MacMillan, New York, pp. 41–42.

Day, G. S., & Fahey, L., 1990, 'Putting Strategy into Shareholder Value Analysis', *Harvard Business Review*, Vol. 68, No. 2, pp. 152–162.

Deeb, G., July 2014, 'Is Your Startup Building a 'Vitamin' or a 'Painkiller'?', *Forbes*, www.forbes.com

Dhalla, N. K., & Yuspeh, S., 1976, 'Forget the Product Life Cycle Concept!', *Harvard Business Review*, Vol. 54, pp. 102–112.

Doerr, J., 2017, *Measure What Matters*, Portfolio Penguin, New York.

Gause, G. F., 1934, *The Struggle for Existence*, The Williams & Wilkins Company, Baltimore.

Goold, M., & Campbell, A., September–October 1998, 'Desperately Seeking Synergy', *Harvard Business Review*, Vol. 76, pp. 131–143.

Grannell, C., 2009, 'Untangling Brand Equity, Value and Health', originally published by brandchannel.com and republished by brandvas.io

Grannell, C., October 2010, *Alignment Is about Getting All Your Little Ducks in a Row*, The Age / Sydney Morning Herald, Nine/ Fairfax Media.

Hauser, J., & Clausing, D., May 1988, 'The House of Quality', *Harvard Business Review*, Vol. 3, pp. 63–73.

Henderson, B., January 1970, *The Product Portfolio*, The Boston Consulting Group, Boston.

Kaplan, R., & Norton, D., January–February 1992, "The Balanced Scorecard – Measures That Drive Performance", *Harvard Business Review*, Vol. 70, pp. 71–79.

Kaplan, R., & Norton, D., September 2000, 'Having Trouble with Your Strategy? Then Map It', *Harvard Business Review*, Vol. 78, No. 5, pp. 167–176.

Keller, K. L., January 1993, 'Conceptualizing, Measuring, and Managing Customer-Based Brand Equity', *Journal of Marketing*, Vol. 57, No. 1, pp. 1–22.

Kerin, R. A. & Peterson, R. A., 1998, *Strategic Marketing Problems: Case and Commands*, Prentice Hall, Upper Saddle River.

Kim, C., & Mauborgne, R., 2004, 'Blue Ocean Strategy', *Harvard Business Review*.

Kim, C., & Mauborgne, R., 2005, 2015, *Blue Ocean Strategy*, Harvard Business Review Press, Brighton, MA.

Kim, C., & Mauborgne, R., 2017, *Blue Ocean Shift*, Hachette, London.

Kotler, P., 1969, *Marketing Management*, Prentice Hall, Upper Saddle River.

Kyriakidi, M., Why and How Should You Measure Brand Equity? Kantar.com. https://www.kantar.com/inspiration/brands/why-and-how-should-you-measure-brand-equity

Lafley, A. G., Martin, R. L., Rivkin, J. W., & Siggelkow, N., 2012, 'Bringing Science to The Art of Strategy', *Harvard Business Review*, Vol. 90, No. 9, pp. 57–66.

Levitt, T., 1960, 'Marketing Myopia', *Harvard Business Review*, Vol. 38, pp. 45–56.

Manning, J., 2021, *Overcoming Floccinaucinihilipilification: Valuing and Monetizing Products and Services,* Pricing Prophets, Melbourne.

Marn, M., & Rosiello, R., September–October 1992, 'Managing Price, Gaining Profit', *Harvard Business Review*, Vol. 70, No. 5, pp. 84–94.

McCarthy, J. E., *Basic Marketing*, various editions from 1960 onwards.

Menon, A., Bharadwaj, S. G., Adidam, P. T., & Edison, S. W., 1999, 'Antecedents and Consequences of Marketing Strategy Making', *Journal of Marketing*, Vol. 63, No. 2, pp. 18–40.

Miles, R., Snow, C., Meyer, A., & Coleman, H., 1978, 'Organizational Strategy, Structure and Process', *Academy of Management Review*, Vol. 3, No. 3, pp. 546–562.

Mokyr, J., 1990, *The Lever of Riches*, Oxford University Press, New York.

Moore, G., 1991, *Crossing the Chasm: Marketing and Selling Technology Products to Mainstream Customers*, HarperCollins, New York.

Morgan, A., 2009, *Eating the Big Fish: How Challenger Brands Can Compete against Brand Leaders*, Wiley, Hoboken.

Olsen, D., 2015, *The Lean Product Playbook*, Wiley, Hoboken.

Osterwalder, A., 2010, *Business Model Generation: A Handbook for Visionaries, Game Changers, and Challengers*, Wiley, Hoboken.

Osterwalder, A. et al., 2014, *Value Proposition Design: How to Create Products and Services Customers Want*, Wiley, Hoboken.

Pendergrast, M., 1993, *For God, Country, and Coca-Cola: The Definitive History of the Great American Soft Drink and the Company That Makes It*, Scribner's, New York.

Peteraf, M., 1993, 'The Cornerstones of Competitive Advantage: A Resource-Based View', *Strategic Management Journal*, Vol. 14, pp. 179–191.

Peters, T., 2011, A Brief History of the 7-S Model, https://tompeters.com/2011/03/a-brief-history-of-the-7-s-mckinsey-7-s-model/.

Peters, T., & Waterman, R., 1982, *In Search of Excellence: Lessons from America's Best Run Companies*, Harper & Row, New York.

Pinker, S., 2011, *The Better Angels of Our Nature*, Viking, New York.

Porras, J., & Collins, J., 1994, Built to Last, HarperCollins. Also featured in Porras, J. & Collins, J., 1996, 'Building Your Company's Vision', *Harvard Business Review*, September–October 1996, pp. 65–77.

Porter, M. E., video interview, YouTube, 30 June 2008, viewed July 2020, http://youtube.com/watch?v=mYF2_FBCvXw.

Porter, M. E., 1979, 'How Competitive Forces Shape Strategy', *Harvard Business Review*, March–April 1979, pp. 137–145.

Porter, M. E., 1980, *Competitive Strategy*, Free Press, New York, pp. 3–5.

Porter, M. E., 1985, *Competitive Advantage: Creating and Sustaining Superior Performance*, Free Press, New York.

Porter, M. E., 1996, 'What Is Strategy?', *Harvard Business Review*, Vol. 74, pp. 61–78.

Porter, M. E., 2001, 'Strategy and the Internet', *Harvard Business Review*, Vol. 79, No. 3, pp. 62–78.

Porter, M. E., 2008, *The Five Competitive Forces That Shape Strategy*, Harvard Business Publishing, Brighton, MA.

Prahalad, C. K., & Hamel, G., 1990, 'The Core Competence of the Corporation', *Harvard Business Review*, Vol. 68, No. 3, pp. 79–91.

Raggio, R., & Leone, B., 2009. 'Chasing Brand Value', *Journal of Brand Management*, Vol. 16, No. 4, pp. 248–263.

Ramanujam, M., & Tacke, G., 2016, *Monetizing Innovation*, Wiley, Hoboken.

Rao, A., Bergen, M., & Davis, S., 2000, 'How to Fight a Price War', *Harvard Business Review*, Vol. 78, No. 2, pp. 107–116.

Ries, A., & Ries, L., 1998, *The 22 Immutable Laws of Branding*, HarperCollins, London.

Ries, E., 2011, *The Lean Startup*, Crown Business, New York.

Rogers, E., 1962, *Diffusion of Innovations*, Free Press, New York.

Rumelt, R., 2017, *Good Strategy / Bad Strategy*, Crown Business, New York.

Srivastava, R. K. et al., January 1998, 'Market-Based Assets and Shareholder Value: A Framework for Analysis', *Journal of Marketing*, Vol. 62, No. 1, pp. 2–18.

Stalk, G., Evans, P., & Shulman, L., 1992, 'Competing on Capabilities', *Harvard Business Review*, March–April 1992.

Suarez, F., & Lanzolla, G., 2005, 'The Half-Truth of First-Mover Advantage', *Harvard Business Review*, Vol. 83, No. 4, pp. 121–127.

Treacy, M., & Wiersema, F., 1997, *The Discipline of Market Leaders: Chose Your Customers, Narrow Your Focus, Dominate Your Market*, Perseus Books, New York.

Ulwick, A., *What Customers Want*. McGraw-Hill, New York.

Van Westendorp, P., 1976, 'NSS-Price Sensitivity Meter (PSM)- A New Approach to Study Consumer Perception of Price', Proceedings of the ESOMAR Congress.

Wack, P., February 1985, 'Scenarios: Uncharted Waters Ahead', *Harvard Business Review*, Vol. 91, No. 5, pp. 118–127.

Waterman, B., Peters, T., & Phillips, J., 1980, 'Structure Is Not Organization', *Business Horizons*, Vol. 23, pp. 14–26.

Index